First World War
and Army of Occupation
War Diary
France, Belgium and Germany

14 DIVISION
Divisional Troops
Divisional Signal Company
19 May 1915 - 31 May 1919

WO95/1890/1

The Naval & Military Press Ltd
www.nmarchive.com
Published in association with The National Archives

Published by

The Naval & Military Press Ltd

Unit 10 Ridgewood Industrial Park,

Uckfield, East Sussex,

TN22 5QE England

Tel: +44 (0) 1825 749494

www.naval-military-press.com

www.nmarchive.com

This diary has been reprinted in facsimile from the original. Any imperfections are inevitably reproduced and the quality may fall short of modern type and cartographic standards.

© Crown Copyright
Images reproduced by permission of The National Archives, London, England, 2015.

Contents

Document type	Place/Title	Date From	Date To
Heading	WO95/1890/1		
Heading	14th Division 14th Signal Coy R.E. May 1915-May 1919		
Heading	14 2w Signals Vol 6		
Heading	14th Division 14th Signal Coy R.E May-Oct 1915 May 19 Vol-I		
War Diary	Havre	19/05/1915	19/05/1915
War Diary	St Omer	20/05/1915	23/05/1915
War Diary	Steenvorde	27/05/1915	27/05/1915
War Diary	Westoutre	31/05/1915	12/06/1915
War Diary	Abeele	14/06/1915	14/06/1915
War Diary	H.7.c.8.2	15/06/1915	10/07/1915
War Diary	Ypres	30/07/1915	03/08/1915
War Diary	H 7 C.8.2	06/08/1915	23/09/1915
War Diary	Ypres	24/09/1915	25/09/1915
War Diary	H 7 C.8.2	26/09/1915	22/10/1915
Diagram etc	43rd Brigade Circuit Diagram.		
Heading	14th Division 14th Signal Coy R.E. Vol 2 Nov 15		
War Diary	H 7 c 8.2	18/11/1915	30/11/1915
Miscellaneous	Relief Of 6th Div. By 14th Div. "A"	19/11/1915	19/11/1915
Miscellaneous	Change Of Command Of 6th & 14th Div. Arty.	19/11/1915	19/11/1915
War Diary	H.7.c.8.2	11/12/1915	31/12/1915
Diagram etc	14 Division Signal Lines		
Diagram etc	Plan Of Forward Lines 14th Division Signal Coy		
Diagram etc			
Miscellaneous	Appendix To Diagram No. 2 14th Divisional Signal Lines "D"		
Miscellaneous	Table Of References		
Miscellaneous	Relief Of 49th-Div By 14th-Div. E		
Heading	14th Signals Vol 4		
War Diary		01/01/1916	31/01/1916
Heading	14th Sig Coy Vol 5		
War Diary	H.7.c.7.7	01/02/1916	20/02/1916
War Diary	Flesselles	22/02/1916	27/02/1916
War Diary	Sus St Leger	28/02/1916	28/02/1916
War Diary	Barly	29/02/1916	01/03/1916
War Diary	Berneville	02/03/1916	12/03/1916
War Diary	Warlus	17/03/1916	30/04/1916
Diagram etc	14th Signal Co.-Diagram Of Lines Of Communication		
Diagram etc	41st Inf Brigade Circuit Diagram		
Miscellaneous	The O.A.G. 3rd Echelon Sterworth War Diary For 14 Signal Coy For Month Of May 1916	03/06/1916	03/06/1916
War Diary	Warlus	01/05/1916	30/06/1916
War Diary	Relief Of 5th Divn By 14th Divn.	19/06/1916	19/06/1916
Heading	14th Signal Company R.E. War Diary For July 1916	02/08/1916	02/08/1916
War Diary	Warlus	01/07/1916	31/07/1916
Heading	14th Division 14th Divisional Signal Company Royal Engineers. August 1916		
War Diary	Bernaville	01/08/1916	06/08/1916
War Diary	Buire-Sur-L'ancre	07/08/1916	08/08/1916

War Diary	Buire	09/08/1916	13/08/1916
War Diary	Albert	14/08/1916	22/08/1916
War Diary	Albert (Bellevue Farm)	23/08/1916	31/08/1916
Diagram etc	14th Signal Co. Forward Exchange System		
Diagram etc	14th Signal Co. Route Map		
Heading	War Diary Of 14th Signal Co R.E. From 1.9.16 To 30.9.16 (Volume 16)	01/10/1916	01/10/1916
War Diary	Fricourt Buire	17/09/1916	21/09/1916
War Diary	Le Cauroy	22/09/1916	22/09/1916
War Diary	Gouy	26/09/1916	26/09/1916
War Diary	Warlus	28/09/1916	28/09/1916
War Diary	Belloy St Leonard	01/09/1916	10/09/1916
War Diary	Buire Fricourt	11/09/1916	13/09/1916
War Diary	Fricourt	15/09/1916	16/09/1916
Miscellaneous	Report On Signal Work During Operations 13th To 17th September 1916 (both Inclusive)	23/09/1916	23/09/1916
Diagram etc	14th Signal Co. Route. Map		
Miscellaneous	Report On Carrier Pigeon Service during attack on 15th and 16th September, 1916	23/09/1916	23/09/1916
Heading	War Diary Of 14th Signal Co R.E. 1st Oct-31st 1916 Volume 17		
War Diary	Warlus	01/10/1916	27/10/1916
War Diary	Le Cauroy	27/10/1916	29/10/1916
Diagram etc	14th Signal Co Diagram Of Divl Lines		
Heading	War Diary Of The 14th Signal Co R.E. From Nov 1st-30th 1916 (Volume 18)		
War Diary		01/11/1916	10/12/1916
Heading	War Diary Of The 14th Signal Company R.E. From 1st Dec To 31st Dec 1916 (Volume 15)		
War Diary	Le Cauroy	01/12/1916	31/12/1916
War Diary		28/12/1916	28/12/1916
Heading	War Diary Of The 14th Signal Company R.E. From 1-31 January 1917 (Volume 16)		
War Diary		01/01/1917	14/01/1917
Heading	War Diary Of The 14th Signal Company R.E. From 1st Feby. 1917-28th Feby. 1917 (Volume 17)		
War Diary	Warlus	03/02/1917	01/03/1917
Heading	War Diary Of The 14th Signal Company R.E. From 1st To 30th April 1917 (Volume 23)	22/05/1917	22/05/1917
Miscellaneous	A.G's Office At The Base.	24/05/1917	24/05/1917
War Diary		01/04/1917	28/04/1917
Diagram etc	Diagram No 1		
Diagram etc	Diagram No 2 41st Infantry Brigade		
Miscellaneous	Notes On Communications During The Offensive 9th-13th April 1917	13/04/1917	13/04/1917
Miscellaneous	14th Division Signal Communications For The Offensive.	02/04/1917	02/04/1917
Miscellaneous	14th Division S.G. 2674	07/04/1917	07/04/1917
Diagram etc	No. 1 Diagram Of Communications Available At Zero		
Diagram etc	No. 2 Diagram Of Communications After Capture Of The Blue Line		
Heading	War Diary Of The 14th Signal Co R.E. From 1st To 31st May 1917 (Volume 24)		
War Diary		01/05/1917	27/05/1917
War Diary		19/05/1917	19/05/1917

Miscellaneous	Scheme For Communications During Forthcoming Operations	02/05/1917	02/05/1917
Diagram etc	Diagram Of Artillery Lines	03/05/1917	03/05/1917
Diagram etc	14th Div Signal Coy		
Heading	War Diary Of The 14th Signal Company R.E. From 1st To 30th June 1917 (Volume-25)		
War Diary		03/06/1917	30/06/1917
War Diary		28/06/1917	28/06/1917
Heading	War Diary Of The 14th Signal Co. R.E. From July 1-31.1917 Volume 26		
War Diary		01/07/1917	31/07/1917
Heading	War Diary Of The 14th Signal Co. R.E. August 1st-31st 1917 Volume 27		
War Diary		01/08/1917	30/08/1917
Miscellaneous	Signal Communications For The Offensive.		
Miscellaneous	Notes On Signal Communications During Operations 22-25 August 1917	30/08/1917	30/08/1917
Heading	War Diary Of The 14th Signal Co RE September 1-30 1917 Volume 28	06/10/1917	06/10/1917
War Diary	Field	01/09/1917	15/09/1917
War Diary	Field	12/09/1917	25/09/1917
War Diary	Field	14/09/1917	29/09/1917
Diagram etc			
Diagram etc	14th Division Buried System		
Heading	War Diary Of The 14th Signal Co R.E. From Oct 1st-Oct 31st 1917 Volume 29	06/11/1917	06/11/1917
War Diary		01/10/1917	30/10/1917
War Diary	Signal Communications In The New Area.	10/10/1917	10/10/1917
Diagram etc	14th Division Visual Communications.		
Diagram etc	14th Division Power Buzzer And Amplifier Communication.		
Heading	War Diary Of The 14th Signal Co. R.E. From 1st Nov To 30th Nov. 1917 Volume 30		
War Diary		01/11/1917	30/11/1917
Heading	War Diary Of The 14th Signal Co. R.E. for December 1917 Volume 31		
War Diary	Wizernes	01/12/1917	31/12/1917
Diagram etc	No 1		
Diagram etc	No 2		
Heading	War Diary Of The 14th Signal Co R.E. From 1st January 1918 To 31st January 1918 Volume 32		
War Diary	Wizernes	02/01/1918	02/01/1918
War Diary	Mericourt Sur Somme	03/01/1918	22/01/1918
War Diary	Guiscard	25/01/1918	25/01/1918
War Diary	Clastres	26/01/1918	31/01/1918
Heading	War Diary Of The 14th Signal Coy. R.E. 1st Feby 1918 To 28th Feby 1918 (Volume 33)		
War Diary	Clastres	04/02/1918	28/02/1918
War Diary		08/02/1918	28/02/1918
Diagram etc	Appendix I		
Heading	14th Divisional Engineers 14th Divisional Signal Company R.E. March 1918		
War Diary	Clastres Ref Sheet 66 CNW Siquentin 18	01/03/1918	22/03/1918
War Diary	Petit Detroit To Stquentin 18	22/03/1918	22/03/1918
War Diary	Beaumonten St Quentin 18	22/03/1918	23/03/1918
War Diary	Guivry St Quentin 18	23/03/1918	24/03/1918

War Diary	Quesmy St Quentin 18	24/03/1918	24/03/1918
War Diary	Crisolley Armies 17	24/03/1917	24/03/1917
War Diary	Lagny Armies 17	24/03/1917	25/03/1917
War Diary	Chiry Armies 17	25/03/1917	26/03/1917
War Diary	Ribercourt Armies 17	26/03/1917	26/03/1917
War Diary	Viller-Sur-Coudun	26/03/1917	26/03/1917
War Diary	Estrees St Denis Beuvais 21	27/03/1917	28/03/1917
War Diary	Sarron Beauvais 21	29/03/1917	29/03/1917
War Diary	Hebecourt Amiens 17	30/03/1917	30/03/1917
Miscellaneous	Notes Of Communications		
Miscellaneous			
Heading	14th Divisional Signal Company. April 1918		
War Diary	Boves (Amiens 17)	01/04/1918	02/04/1918
War Diary	Aubigny	03/04/1918	04/04/1918
War Diary	Fouilloy	04/04/1918	04/04/1918
War Diary	Glisy	05/04/1918	05/04/1918
War Diary	St Fuscien	07/04/1918	12/04/1918
War Diary	Hucqueliers	14/04/1918	15/04/1918
War Diary	Ecquedecques	15/04/1918	15/04/1918
War Diary	Laires	16/04/1918	18/04/1918
War Diary	Wambercourt	19/04/1918	19/04/1918
War Diary	Fressin	21/04/1918	21/04/1918
War Diary	Coyecque	22/04/1918	29/04/1918
Heading	War Diary Of The 14th Divisional Signal Coy. R.E. For. May 1918 Volume. 36		
War Diary	Lebiez	01/05/1918	12/05/1918
War Diary	Moulin Le Comte	13/05/1918	31/05/1918
Heading	War Diary Of The 14th Signal Coy R.E. June 1918 Volume 37		
War Diary	Moulin Le Comte	01/06/1918	07/06/1918
War Diary	Moulin Le Comte	01/06/1918	30/06/1918
Miscellaneous	H.Q. 14th (Light) Division, G.	14/06/1918	14/06/1918
Miscellaneous	14th (Light) Division. Scheme Of Communication For The Manning Of The Lillers-Steenbecque Line.		
Heading	War Diary Of The 14th Signal Coy R.E. 1st July 1918-31st July 1918 (Volume 34)		
War Diary	Moulin Le Comte	01/07/1918	05/07/1918
War Diary	Setques	06/07/1918	06/07/1918
War Diary	Wierre Effroy	07/07/1918	11/07/1918
War Diary	Eperlecques	12/07/1918	31/07/1918
Miscellaneous	Arrangements For Signal Communications Winnezeele Line.	20/07/1918	20/07/1918
Heading	War Diary Of The 14th Signal Coy R.E. August 1918 (Volume 39)		
War Diary	Eperlecques	01/08/1918	19/08/1918
War Diary	Couthovc	20/08/1918	31/08/1918
Heading	War Diary Of The 14th Divisional Signal Coy. R.E. From. 1st September-30th September 1918		
War Diary	Couthove	01/09/1918	19/09/1918
War Diary	Orwell Camp	20/09/1918	27/09/1918
War Diary	Hague Fm H 31a.7.9	28/09/1918	29/09/1918
War Diary	Waratah	30/09/1918	30/09/1918
Heading	War Diary Of The 14 Divisional Signal Coy RE Period October 1918		
War Diary	Waratah	01/10/1918	01/10/1918
War Diary	Kandahar F M 28/T106.B.8.8	02/10/1918	05/10/1918

War Diary	Kandahar F M	05/10/1918	17/10/1918
War Diary	Wervicq	18/10/1918	18/10/1918
War Diary	Blanc Four	19/10/1918	20/10/1918
War Diary	Mouscron	21/10/1918	03/11/1918
War Diary	Tourcoing	04/11/1918	31/05/1919

(1) 1890/1895

(1) 1890/1945

14TH DIVISION

14TH SIGNAL COY R.E.

MAY 1915 - MAY 1919

14 Luu
Segnale
vol 6

12/7594

14th Battalion

14th Signal Coy RE.

Oct:
May —— ~~Septbr~~ '9.5,

May 1/9
Vol - I

Army Form C. 2118.

WAR DIARY
or
INTELLIGENCE SUMMARY.
(Erase heading not required.)

Instructions regarding War Diaries and Intelligence Summaries are contained in F. S. Regs., Part II. and the Staff Manual respectively. Title pages will be prepared in manuscript.

Place	Date	Hour	Summary of Events and Information	Remarks and references to Appendices
HAVRE	19/5/15	9.30 AM	Company disembarked - completed by 4 PM. Entrained 11.30 PM	
ST OMER	20/5/15	11.30 PM	Company detrained and marched to Billets at WATTEN arriving there 3.30 AM 21st. Division HQ established at manufactory. Opened Telegraphic Communication with the 41st and 42nd Brigades at MILLAIN and BOLLEZEELE respectively	
"	23rd		43rd Brigade Section arrived and Billetts at NEDERZEEL. Communication established	
STEEN-VORDE	27/k		Division Sig opened at 11.30 AM. Brigades Billetted at EECKE CAESTRE FLETRE and R.A at STRAZEELE	
WESTOUTRE	31st	6 AM	HQ moved here with Advanced Report Centre at OUDERDOM. Took over 3rd Divs lines. Advanced report centre used during day with night HQ at WESTOUTRE	
"				

E.W.S.Balfour Major
Cmdg 14th Signal Coy R.E.

1st June 1915

Army Form C. 2118.

WAR DIARY
or
INTELLIGENCE SUMMARY.
(Erase heading not required.)

Instructions regarding War Diaries and Intelligence Summaries are contained in F. S. Regs., Part II. and the Staff Manual respectively. Title pages will be prepared in manuscript.

Place	Date	Hour	Summary of Events and Information	Remarks and references to Appendices
WESTOUTRE	1 June		Company still working and maintaining same system of wires	
	4 "		Advanced Div HQ at OUDERDON closed for good.	
	6 "		41st Bde relieved 85th Bde and took over their lines	
	12 "		84th " relieved 41st Bde who moved into rest.	
ABEELE	14 "		Division handed over to 20th Div, who took over existing lines. Div HQ established in farm L 13 b 4 . 6	
H7c 8.2	15 "		Divisional HQ moved to WEAZEL HERBERGE. Communication established with 3rd Division in YPRES, V Corps at ABEELE and all Brigades.	
	16 "		Attack by 3rd Division on Railway Wood. 42nd Bde move up in Support.	
	18 "		Orders received for Division to remain in present quarters. Remainder of Division moved up	
	19 R		42nd Bde took over portion of line and established Signal Office in ECOLE near Ramparts YPRES	
	24 "		43rd Bde relieved 42nd Bde in ECOLE.	
	25 "		Sergt O'Hara (of No 4 Section) killed. The first casualty in the Company.	
	26 "		43rd Bde shelled out of ECOLE and fell back into YPRES, taking over the Office	

WAR DIARY
or
INTELLIGENCE SUMMARY.

Second sheet

(Erase heading not required.)

Army Form C. 2118.

Place	Date	Hour	Summary of Events and Information	Remarks and references to Appendices
H.Q.C.P.2	28 June		which was being prepared for advanced Div: Hd. Party of Officers arrived from England for attachment.	
	30 "		O.C. N°2 Section gassed. All lines working well	
	5 July		Germans rushed barricade in Railway Wood, but were bombed out. Tried to get up signals by means of earth, new German lines. Stayed all night. Picked up British signals but no German ones.	
	10 "		Took over sector on Right embracing HOOGE	
YPRES	30 "	3.20pm	Germans started heavy bombardment and liquid fire attack. Part of Trenches rushed near HOOGE. Brigade Hq moved to ZOUAVE WOOD. Advanced Div Hd moved to Ramparts YPRES. Counter attack 2.45 pm only partially successful. All lines held and worked splendidly. Casualties heavy	
	31 "		Enemy continued heavy shelling and attempted another attack. 41st Bde relieved by 43rd Bde on night of 30/31. Owing to enemy activity 6th Division sent up 1 Brigade to reinforce. An advanced line but all lines held. Had perfect talking circuit from Div Hd to Battalions in the Trenches	

1.8.15.

R.W. Ball R.E. Major

Army Form C. 2118.

WAR DIARY
or
INTELLIGENCE SUMMARY.
(Erase heading not required.)

Instructions regarding War Diaries and Intelligence Summaries are contained in F. S. Regs., Part II. and the Staff Manual respectively. Title pages will be prepared in manuscript.

Place	Date	Hour	Summary of Events and Information	Remarks and references to Appendices
YPRES	1 Aug		HQ very heavily shelled. Several Casualties in the Company.	
	3 "		O.C. 6 Div Signals taken round and showed our dug-outs.	
H7c 8.2	6 "		Div. HQ moved back to HERBERGE DE WEAZEL	
	7 "		Went round & see all lines in working order which had been handed over to the 6th Div Signals. Sent Linemen to Latter Company to assist	
	9 "		VI Division retook HOOGE. all lines (same) to VI Div worked well and gave no trouble	
	19 "		Started a Signal School at SAN JAN TER BIEZEN for instruction of Operators and Linemen.	
	25 "		Surveyed new lines for projected Operations and arranged for construction	

1 Sept 15.

J.W. Becker
Major
Cmdg 1st 4th Signal Coy

1577 Wt. W10791/1773 500,000 1/15 D. D. & L. A.D.S.S./Forms/C. 2118.

Army Form C. 2118.

WAR DIARY
or
INTELLIGENCE SUMMARY.
(Erase heading not required.)

Instructions regarding War Diaries and Intelligence Summaries are contained in F. S. Regs., Part II. and the Staff Manual respectively. Title pages will be prepared in manuscript.

Place	Date	Hour	Summary of Events and Information	Remarks and references to Appendices
H 7 c 8.2	23 Sep		Tested all new lines and found them working well. Brigade (42nd) moved to Advanced HQ.	
YPRES	24 "	AM	Divisn HQ moved into Ramparts YPRES. Weather very much against good communication.	
	25 "	3.50	Bombardment commenced. Trenches captured from Germans then lost. 43rd Bde relieved 42nd during night. Div HQ very heavily shelled.	
H 7 c 8.2	26 "		Div. HQ moved back to ordinary HQ.	
	28 "		43rd Bde HQ blown in by 17" shell. Whole office wrecked. Men very much shaken, but only one wounded. Changed HQ to KAAIE SALIENT.	
	22.04		Division moved into Rest.	

17.XI.15

[signature]
O/C 14th Signal Coy

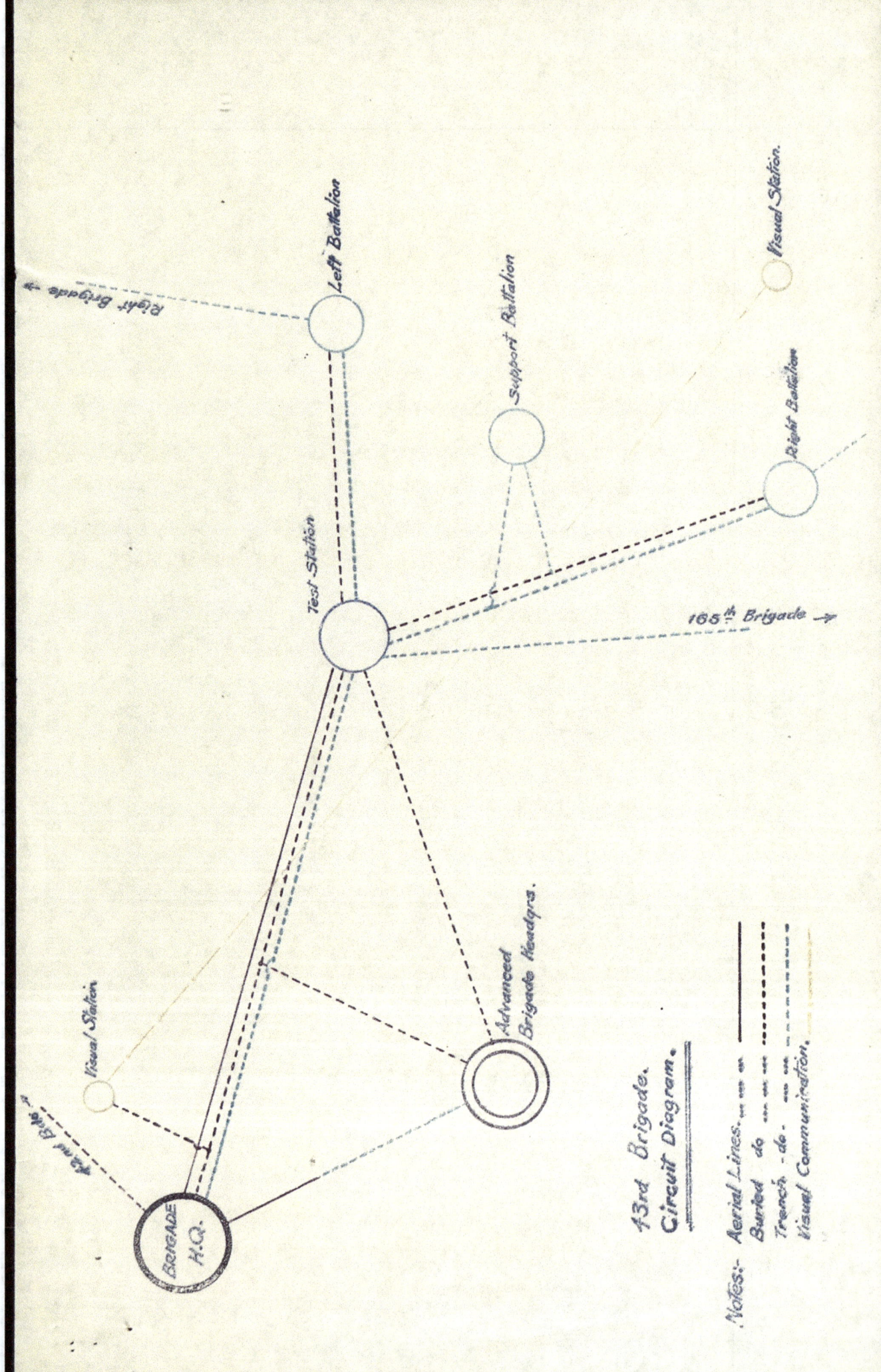

14th Burman

14th Signal Coy RE.
Vol: 2

1/2/
7656

Nov 15

Army Form C. 2118

WAR DIARY
or
INTELLIGENCE SUMMARY.
(Erase heading not required.)

Instructions regarding War Diaries and Intelligence Summaries are contained in F. S. Regs., Part II. and the Staff Manual respectively. Title pages will be prepared in manuscript.

Place	Date	Hour	Summary of Events and Information	Remarks and references to Appendices
H7 C.8.2	Nov 18th		41st and 43rd Brigades went back into the line relieving the 16th and 18th Brigades respectively. Orders for change attached - marked "A"	Order for change - "A"
"	"	7.45 AM	Div. H.Q. bombed - damage nil.	
		11.0 AM	Great German Aeroplane activity.	
"	19th	9.55 PM	Switches lines over as shown in "A"&"B" attached, on the G.O.C. 14th Div. assuming Command vice 6th Division to Rest. 43rd Bde. took over from 71st I.B.	"B"
		10 PM	All new lines running smoothly. 14th R.A. took over from 6th Div. R.A.	
"	20/21	night		
"	21/22			
"	25th	7 PM	41st & 43rd Brigade HQ heavily shelled. 2/Lt Kay O.C. No. 4 Signal Section wounded.	
"	30		New Advanced Div. Office established at H.5 c.9.9, but not occupied.	

Candy Major
O/C No. 14 Signal Co.

14th SIGNAL COMPANY
30 Nov 1915
R.E.

Copy No. ....

"A"

RELIEF OF 6ᵀᴴ DIV. by 14ᵀᴴ DIV.

The following alterations in Infantry Lines will take place at 9.55 ᵃ·ᵐ· on the 19ᵀᴴ November 1915.

Unit going in.	Unit coming out.	Nature of Line.	Rear portion of Line.	Forward portion of Line.	Joined up at.
41ˢᵗ Inf. Bde. Signal Office.	18ᵗʰ Inf. Bde. Signal Office in C.25.d.2.4.	Telephone pair.	F.48 a. and b. (YN-YF pair)	3ᵃ (Lead pair.)	Y.F.
		Vibrator Line.	F.B. 32	2ᵃ	S.J.
42ⁿᵈ Inf. Bde. Signal Office.	16ᵗʰ Inf. Bde. Signal Office in I.2.c.0.9	Telephone pair.	Spare. † (HAR-YF pair)	F.33 a. and b.	YF. dugout.
		Vibrator Line.	F.B. 34	L.Z. 31.	G.C.
43ʳᵈ Inf. Bde. Signal Office.	71ˢᵗ Inf. Bde. Signal Office in C.25.d.3.6	Telephone pair.	HAR-YF pair. †	3ᵃ * (twisted D.5. pair)	YF.
		Vibrator Line.	YN. 1	3 *	YF.

N.B. YN 2. will be joined to YF.—YD1. vibrator line at YF.

† These lines now extend back to YN.
* These lines must also be put through at 6ᵗʰ Div. Advᵈ HQ.

Issued at :- 11.45. ᵃ·ᵐ·

Copies to :-
- No 1 — 14ᵗʰ Div. Staff (for information)
- " 2 — 6ᵗʰ Corps Signals.
- " 3 — 41ˢᵗ Brigade "
- " 4 — 42ⁿᵈ " "
- " 5 — 43ʳᵈ " "
- " 6 — 6ᵗʰ Div Signals.
- " 7 — O.C. No 1 Section.
- " 8 — S.J. Test Office.
- " 9 — G.C. " "
- " 10 — File

E.J.W. Barker
Major,
O.C. 14ᵗʰ Signal Co
18ᵗʰ November 1915.

Copy No. "B"

19th November 1915.

Change of Command of 6th & 14th Div. Arty.

The following alterations in Artillery Lines will take place at 9.55 a.m. 19. Nov. 1915.

Unit.	Rear portion of Line.	Forward portion of Line.	Nature of Line	Joined up at:-
2nd R.F.A. Brigade	FYN.2	4	Vibrator Line.	SJ.
24th -do- -do-	*FYN.3	1	-do- -do-	SJ.
12th -do- -do-	F.28 (YN-YF Vibr Line)	2 (rear portion)	-do- -do-	YF.
Heavy Howitzer Group	FYN.4	Heavy Howitzer Line.	-do- -do-	YF.

* Now extended to FYN.

Issued at 3.0 a.m.

Copies to:-

No 1 14th Div Staff (for information.)
 " 2 C.R.A. (for information.)
 " 3 6th Corps Signals.
 " 4 2nd R.F.A. Brigade.
 " 5 24th -do- -do-
 " 6 12th -do- -do-
 " 7 6th Div. Signals.
 " 8 O.C. No. 1 Section
 " 9 S.J. Test Office.
 " 10 File.
 " 11 Heavy Howitzer Group.

C.H.W. Barkes, Major
O.C. 14th Div. Signal Co.

Army Form C. 2118.

WAR DIARY
or
INTELLIGENCE SUMMARY.
(Erase heading not required.)

Place	Date	Hour	Summary of Events and Information	Remarks and references to Appendices
H 7 c 8.2	11 Dec	3 AM	Signal dug out at Battalion HQ blown in and Operator wounded	
"	16 "	9.55 AM	Lines to all Infantry Brigades handed over to 6th Division in relief	
		12.55 PM	" " Artillery " " " " " "	
			Average number of Despatches etc dealt with daily when all Brigades are in the line :-	
			Telegrams 926.2	
			Despatches 389.86	
			Telephone Calls 235.8	
			Total daily average 1551.86	
	17 "		Division in Rest. Diagrams showing all the Circuits in use at time	Diagrams Nos 2, 3 & 4 & Appendices
			of handing over to 6th Division, and Office diagram attached and marked "A B C & D" and numbered 2, 3, 4 and "appendix"	
	19 "	5.35 AM	Gas attack —	
	25 "	4 PM	All orders as to prospective move cancelled	
	30 "	9.55 AM	Took over lines from 49th Division. Plan of relief attached marked "E".	E
	31 "		Lines 6th Brigade working well, but forward to Battalions in very bad state.	

J.W.R. McGrigor
Cmdg No 10 Signals

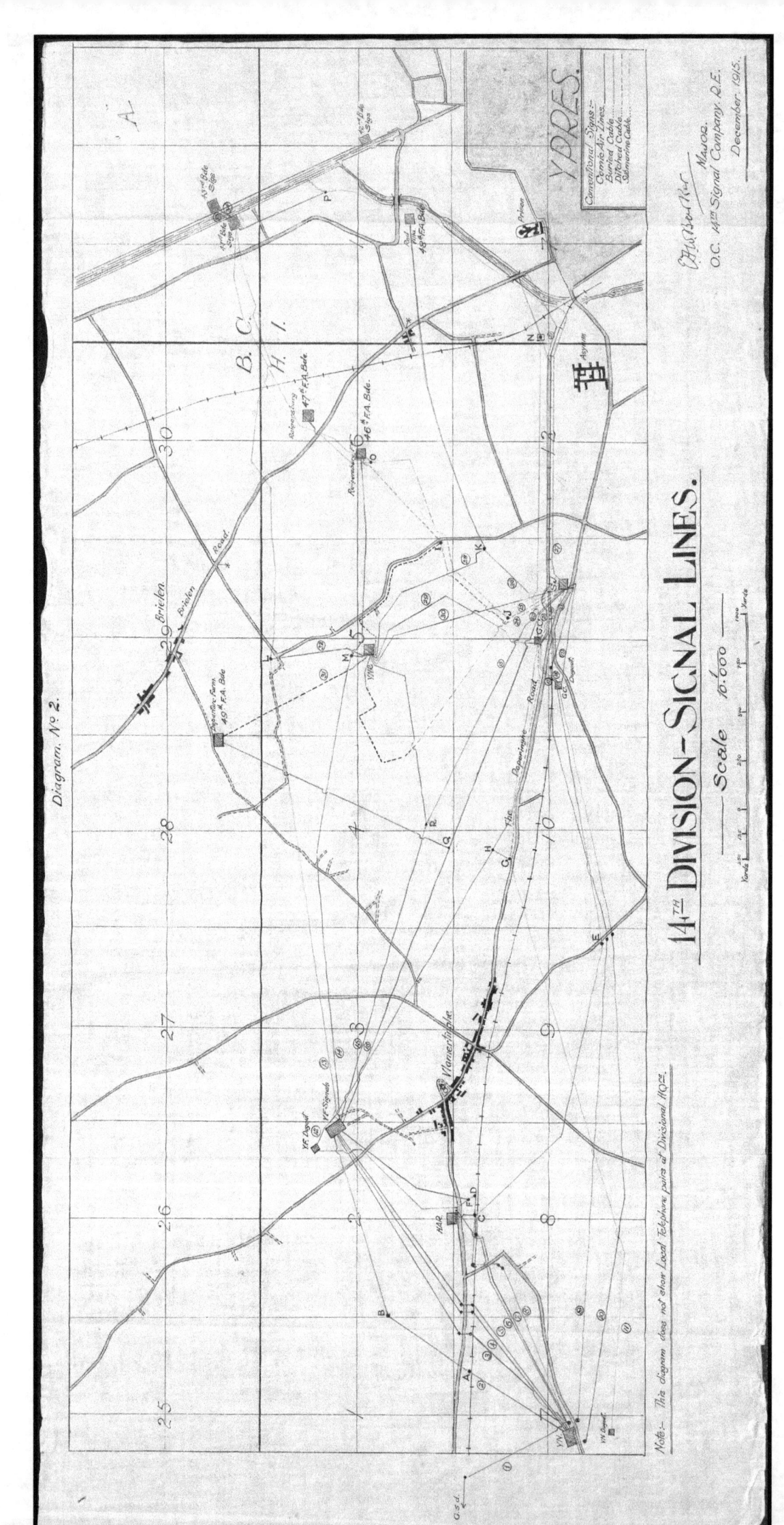

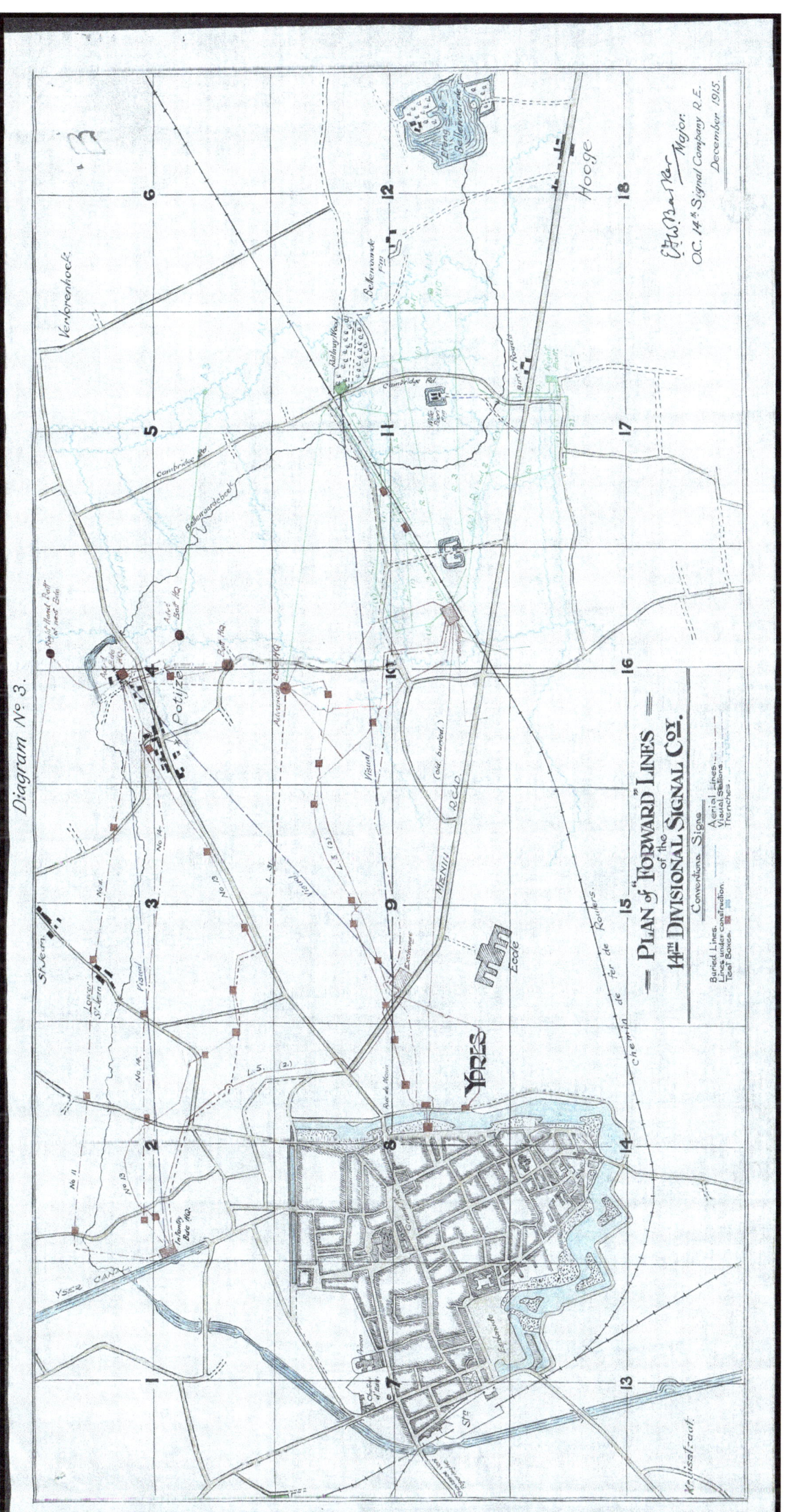

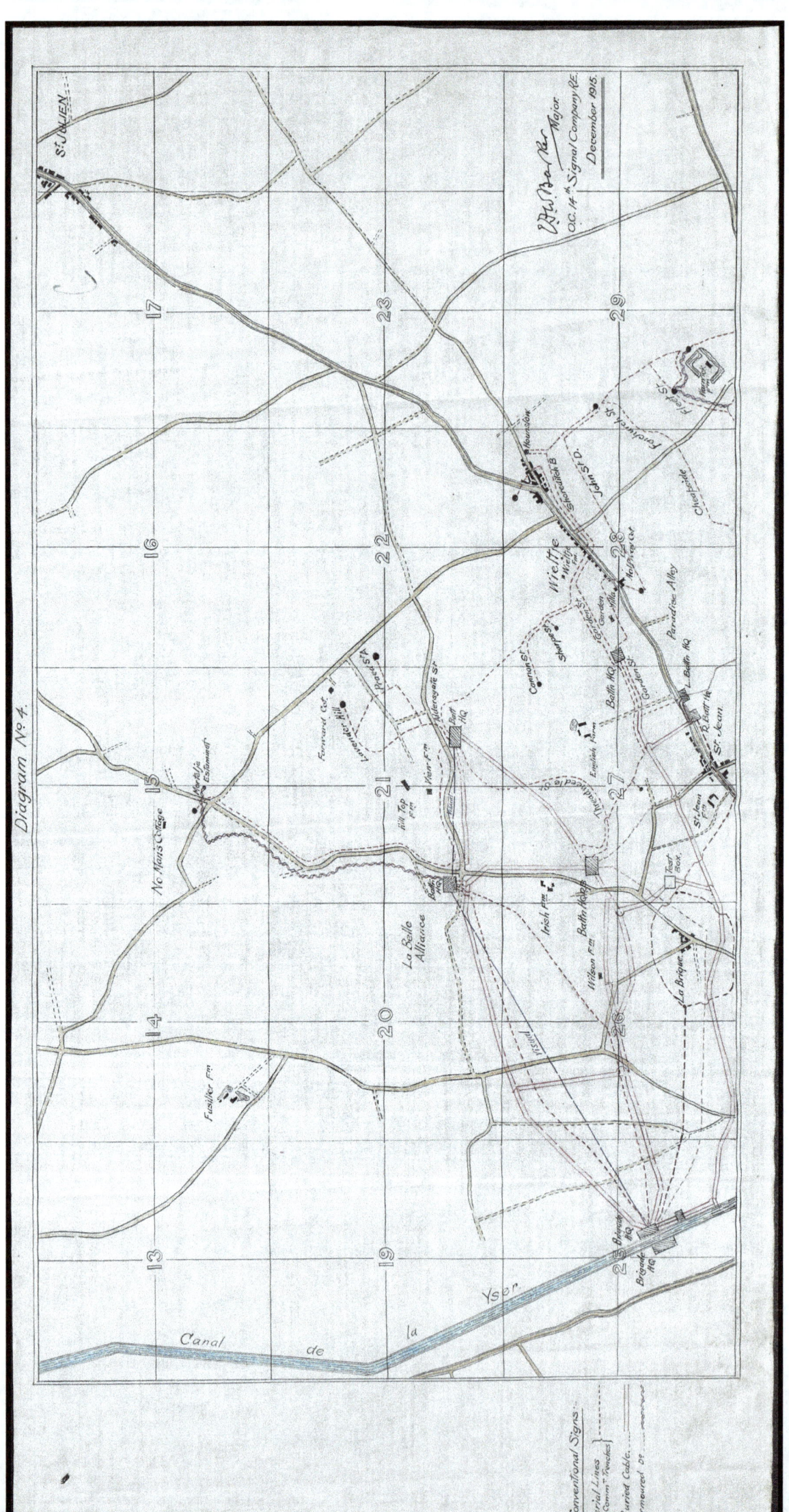

"D"

APPENDIX
-- to --
Diagram No. 2.

14th DIVISIONAL SIGNAL LINES.
----------oOo----------

This Diagram is intended to show approximately the routes available for telegraphic and telephonic communication between the 14th Divisional Headquarters, and its Brigades, both Infantry and Artillery.

Lateral communications to neighbouring Divisions should be dealt with by the Corps: Those to neighbouring Brigades are shown in the diagrams of forward lines.

The lines in use up to Artillery Brigades, viz ;

                    F Y N 1
                    F Y N 2
                    F Y N 3
                    F Y N 4
                    F Y N 5
                      F 55

are normally extended back to the Artillery Signal Office, 200 yards due West of Y.N. (This is not shown on accompanying diagram).

TABLE of REFERENCES

Ref. No.	Line No.	From	To	Joined to.	At	No. of wires on Route	Remarks
①	-	YN	G.5.d (sht. 28)	-	-	1	Available for reserve Bde. or Transports
②	F.28	YN	YF	⑮	YF	3	Single line only between 'A' & 'B' Working as FYN 5
③	F 48 a & b / F 52 a & b	YN / YN	YF / outside HAR	⑬	YF) / -)	4	spare.
④	F 38	YN	YF	⑭	YF	1	-
⑤	F 39	YN	YF	YDIR line	YF	1	working as an inter-divnl. line
⑥	L L 25	YN	HAR	-	-	1	-
⑦	F 51 a & b	YN	outside HAR	-	-	2	spare.
⑧	F 56) / F 33 a) / FYN 4) /) / F 33 b)	YN / YN / YN / / as	GC / YF dug-out / YF / / F 33 a	⑰ / ⑫ / 33rd Hy.Bde.	GC dug-out) / YF dg.out) /) YF) /) /)	4	F 56 runs from 'C' as top of 4 line route F 56) F 54 a&b) F 53) to 'E' and thence in same trench with them to G C dug-out. F 33 a&b run fm. 'D' as 2-comic FYN 4 runs as poled cable from F to YF. 33rd Heavy Bde. line runs to A 22 (ref.sheet 28) (not shown on diagram)
⑨	FYN 1) / FYN 2) / FYN 3)	YN	SJ	㉖ / ㉓ / ㉔	SJ	3	-
⑩	F 49 a) / F 55) / F 49 b)	YN	GC dugout	⑱) / ⑲) / ⑯)	GC dug-out	3	-

Ref. No.	Line No.	From	To	Joined to	At	No. of wires on route	Remarks.
(11)	FB 32) FB 34)	YN	GC	(22)	GC	2	Wires diverge at 'G', FB 32 going to 'H' where it joins spare D5 in (12) route to GC. FB 34 runs from 'G' to 'GC' in road ditch (spare). N.B. Owing to induction troubles it would be advisable to abandon portion of FB 32 forward of 'G' and bunch back portion at that point with FB 34 as a single line.
(12)	F33 a & b) Spare D 5)	YF dugout	GC	(20)	GC)	3	F33 a & b is lead cable. From 'H' forward D5 is in use as FB 32.
(13)	3A (YF lead) 3A (YF D5)	YF	41st Bde (In use by 49th Division)	-	-)	4	'L' in junction for looping in YNR
(14)	4A (YF)	YF	41st Bde	(34)	41st Bde.	2	Pair is bunched for telegraph working 'teed' into YNR at 'M'
(15)	2A rear (YF)	YF	YNR	F7*	YF	1	* not shown. Teed into SJ from 'R'
(16)	2 (YF)	YF	SJ	"	-	1	Teed into 49th F.A. Bde. from 'Q'
(17)	-	GC dugout	GC	(23)	GC	1	--
(18)	-	"	"	(21)	GC	2	--
(19)	-	"	SJ	(25)	SJ	1	--

Ref No.	Line No.	From	To	Joined to	At	No. of wires on route	Remarks
20	FB 61 a & b) F 62	GC	42nd Bde	-	-	3	FB 61 a & b is load cable. F 62 working to 'N' as loop on LZ 31. Spare from N forward
21	-	GC	PRISON	-	-	2	Working to Town Major YPRES.
22	LZ 31	GC	42nd Bde	-	-	1	Blocked under flange of North rail of Railway.
23	-	GC	SJ	-	-	3	1 line joined to 2A forward (YF) 2 spare.
24	4 (YF)	SJ	46th FA Bde	-	-	1	Teed into YNR from I.
25	1 (YF)	SJ	47th FA Bde	-	-	1	Teed into YNR from J " " 46th FA Bde from O.
26	FYN 1 & 2 spare D5	SJ	48th F.A. Bde.	-	-	3	FYN 1 & 2 is load cable. Junction box at K for looping into YNR
27	2A forward YF	SJ	41st Bde	-	-	1	Auxiliary loop from 'P' to 41st Bde.
28	FYN 1 & 2 Extn.loop	'K'	YNR	-	-	4	Normally out of circuit
29	F 33 a & b) extn.) FB 61 a & b) extn.)	GC	YNR	-	-	4	Normally out of circuit.
30	LZ 31 extn) 2A forward) extn.) spare D5)	SJ	YNR	-	-	3	Normally out of circuit.
31	-	YNR	48th FA Bde.	-	-	1	-
32	3A (YF lead) extn.	'L'	YNR	-	-	2	Normally out of circuit.
33	-	41st Bde	43rd Bde	-	-	2	Extension on 3A (YF lead) Normally in circuit.
34	-	41st Bde	43rd Bde	-	-	1	Extn. on 4A (YF) bunched. This line is not in use by 41st Bde.

Copy No. **E**

Relief of 49TH Div by 14TH Div.

The following alterations in Infantry and Artillery Lines will take place at 9.55 AM on the 30th inst.

Unit coming in.	Unit going out.	Nature of Line.	Rear portion of Line	Forward portion of Line	Joined up at
41st Inf. Bde Signal Office.	148th Inf. Bde Signal Office.	Vibrator.	F.38 / 7	7 / ZNH Line	YF. YDIR.
"	"	Telephone pair	F.33 a.& b.	ZNH pair	YF Dugout.
42nd Inf. Bde Signal Office	147th Inf. Bde Signal Office	Morse intermediate line	73 / 64 b	64 b / ZNG	Junction Rd YF YDIR.
"	"	Telephone pair	(To terminate at YDIR on Exchange) 71 a & b	63 a & b	Junction Rd YF
43rd Inf. Bde Signal Office	146th Inf. Bde Signal Office	Vibrator.	F.55.	YF 3	S.J.
"	"	Telephone pair	48 a. & b	YF 3b Twisted D5 pr	YF.
14th Div Artillery to YDIR		Morse Line	F.70	YF – YDIR vib^r Line	YF.
		Telephone pr	F.52 a & b	YF – YDIR	YF. Dugout.

Issued at :– 6.0 P.M.

Copies to :–
- No 1. 14th Div Staff (for information.)
- 2. 14th D.A. – do –
- 3. 6th Corps Signals.
- 4. 41st Bde "
- 5. 42nd Bde "
- 6. 43rd Bde "
- 7. 49th Div "
- 8. O.C N^o1 Sec "
- 9. 6th Div. Signals.
- 10. File
- 11. D.A. Signals.

W.R.Parker /
Major
14th Div. Signal Co
29th December. 1915.

14th Sepiah
vol 4

Army Form C. 2118.

WAR DIARY
or
INTELLIGENCE SUMMARY.
(Erase heading not required.)

Instructions regarding War Diaries and Intelligence Summaries are contained in F. S. Regs., Part II. and the Staff Manual respectively. Title pages will be prepared in manuscript.

Place	Date	Hour	Summary of Events and Information	Remarks and references to Appendices
1916 1st Jan.	—	—	Nothing to report. Company & Brigade section	
6 "			Line slightly extended and 4/3rd Bde Section took over extra lines	
16 "			Corps started to lay 'Comic Bn' line from proposed new Div HQ	
21 "			Army Curtin Section commenced to build permanent route from proposed new Div HQ to Advanced Report Centre	
26 "			No: 517 wounded at ZZB	
27 "			Ponjaw Pavate at ZZA wounded	
31 "			Nothing to report.	

1st Feb 16

AMMcManan
Cmdg 14th Signal Coy

14 a Sig Coy
Vol 5

Army Form C. 2118.

Instructions regarding War Diaries and Intelligence Summaries are contained in F. S. Regs., Part II. and the Staff Manual respectively. Title pages will be prepared in manuscript.

WAR DIARY
or
INTELLIGENCE SUMMARY.
(Erase heading not required.)

Place	Date	Hour	Summary of Events and Information	Remarks and references to Appendices
H7c7.7	1st Feb		Nothing to report.	
-do-	4th "	12 noon	6th Corps relieved by 14th Corps	
-do-	10th "		41st Bde withdrawn from line. Changes effected as shown on attached Appendix marked "A".	
	11		Corporal (MC) Hoad killed near Poperinghe. All lines down to Corps from shelling of Poperinghe. 20th Division begun to take over. 42nd Inf Bde relieved by 60th Inf Bde. Changes shown on "A" attached.	
	12		43rd Inf Bde relieved by 59th Inf Bde. Heavy shelling all along the front. All lines held inspite of bombardment.	
	13		Div: HQ at H7c 7.7 closed down at 10.30 AM and reopened same hour at ESQUELBECQ. Signal Office in the CHATEAU	
	15		Div: RA HQ closed at H7c 7.7 at 6 AM and reopened at ZEGGERS CAPPEL same time.	
	19th "		No 1 Section Y Hills entrained at CASSEL at 10.31 PM. Y left for Flesselles	
	20th "		detrained at LONGUEAU near AMIENS. Proceeded by march to Flesselles proceeded by march

Army Form C. 2118.

WAR DIARY
or
INTELLIGENCE SUMMARY.
(Erase heading not required.)

Second Sheet

Place	Date	Hour	Summary of Events and Information	Remarks and references to Appendices
FLESSELLES	22nd		Route to FLESSELLES. Arrived there 2.30 P.M. Opened office in CHATEAU. 131st Bde established their HQ at FLESSELLES and the 142nd Bde at BERTEAUCOURT. The Divisional RA established their HQ at BELLOY SUR SOMME on 20th and Communication opened by cable at 5 PM on 21st.	
	23rd	6pm	Named tomorrow off at 9 AM next day.	
	24th		Marched to DOULLENS. Roads very difficult owing to ice. Billetted at in the Town.	
	25th		Marched to SUS-ST-LEGER (see sheet 11). Very difficult march owing to state of roads & heavy flurry and the white way. Lorry made trip-through.	
	26th		Halt to division to collect its transport which was unable to get through owing to the state of Roads. Lorry brought in during afternoon.	
	27th		Went forward to reconnoitre French lines belonging to the 33rd French Division whose HQ were at BERNEVILLE with one Brigade in ARRAS and the other in DAINVILLE	

Army Form C. 2118.

WAR DIARY
or
INTELLIGENCE SUMMARY.

Third Sheet

(Erase heading not required.)

Place	Date	Hour	Summary of Events and Information	Remarks and references to Appendices
SUS ST LEGER	28th		Sent advance party of Linemen under Sgt Watkins forward from with the French Company marched to BARLY CHATEAU	
BARLY	29th		and opened Office in GRAND CHATEAU	

Berneville
4th March 1916

E.H.D. Res Major
Cmdg 1st R Signal Coy

WAR DIARY
or
INTELLIGENCE SUMMARY.

(Erase heading not required.)

Army Form C. 2118.

Reference Map "Lens Sheet II." First chief.

Place	Date	Hour	Summary of Events and Information	Remarks and references to Appendices
	March			
BARLY	1st		Division remained stationary. Went forward to reconnoitre French Lines.	
BERNEVILLE	2nd		Took over from the French at 10 A.M. No hitch. G.O.C. XIV British Division assumed Command of Line in relief of G.O.C. 33rd French Division. Lines working satisfactorily. 41st Inf Bde in ARRAS, 43rd Inf Bde in DAINVILLE. Signal Office established in the "Mairie". Billets and Office fitly henceforward to be disinfected.	
	3rd		Company fully employed in straightening up lines & patrolling.	
	4th		Heavy blizzard brought down most of the aerial lines. Kept communication chiefly through underground wires.	
	5th		Division front re-arranged. 4/2 WSB put into the line between 41st and 43rd Bdes. Headquarters in ARRAS.	
	9th		Bde Corporal Wounded when repairing lines in ARRAS	
	12th		Pte Heaves on to Company Exchange in Gendarmerie.	
WARLUS	17th	2 P.M	Divisional HQ shifted from Berneville and reopened in Warlus. R.A. H.Q. remaining in Berneville	
"	23rd	3 A.M	R.A. H.Q. join up with Div H.Q. in Warlus at 3 A.M.	

EDWilson Major
Cmdg 14th Signal [Co]

Army Form C. 2118.

WAR DIARY
or
INTELLIGENCE SUMMARY.
(Erase heading not required.)

Instructions regarding War Diaries and Intelligence Summaries are contained in F. S. Regs., Part II. and the Staff Manual respectively. Title pages will be prepared in manuscript.

Place	Date	Hour	Summary of Events and Information	Remarks and references to Appendices
WARLUS	1915 1st Ap	—	Nothing to report	
— '' —	20		H.Q. Bde HQ shelled. G.O.C. moved into another street in RUE CAPUCHIN	
''	22nd		Hd changed to RUE DES FOURS	
''	30th		Nothing to report.	
			Circuit diagrams of Brigade sections attached. Also one of the Division	

30/4/16.

D.H. Wilson. Major.
O in C XIV Signal Coy

(Stamp: 14th SIGNAL COMPANY No. Vol 1 R.E.)

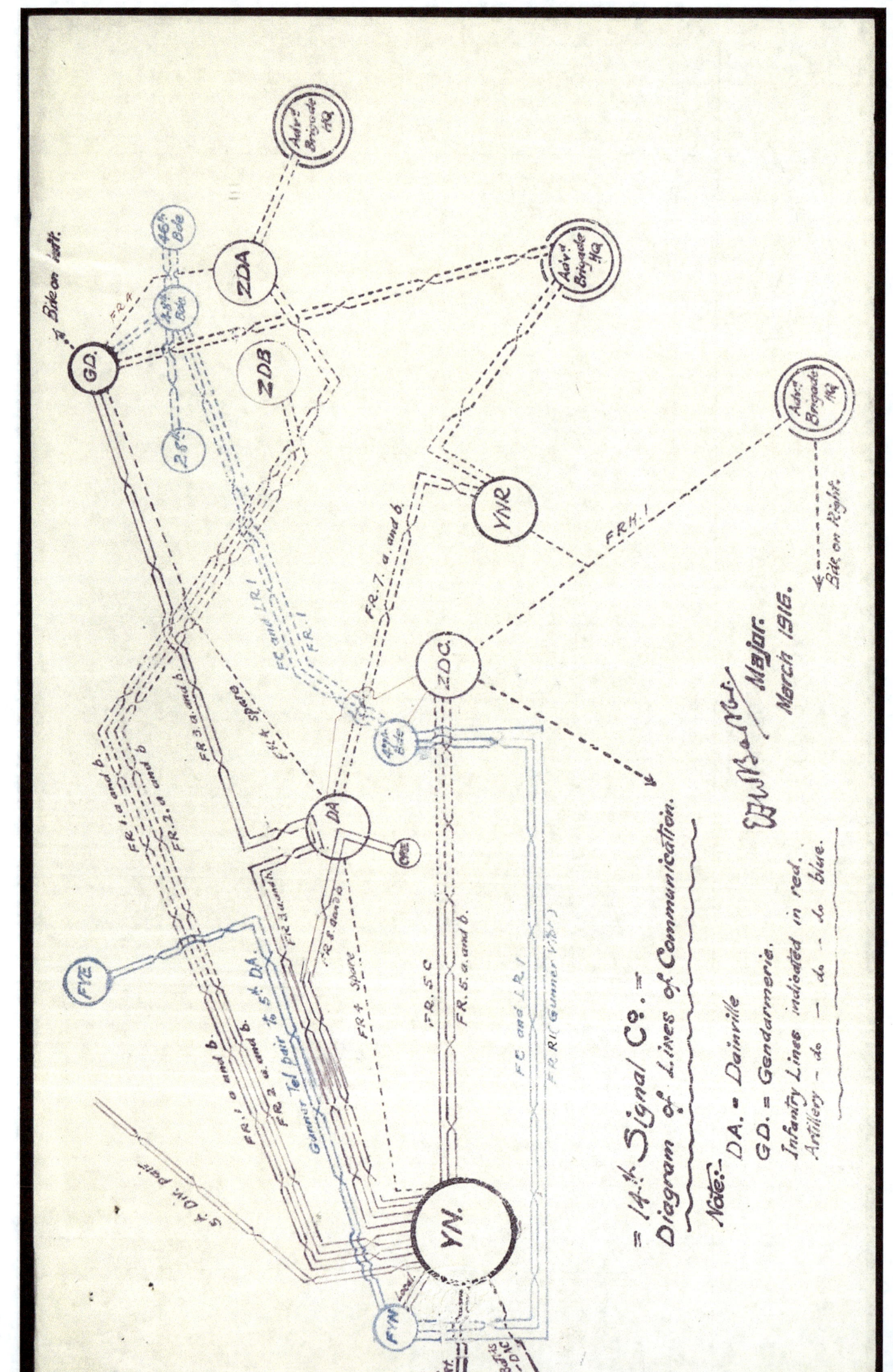

41st Inf. Brigade Circuit Diagram.

Notes:— Power Circuits
Aerial Lines.
Buried . do .
Trench . do .
Junctions marked * have been joined up to main Sewer.

The O.i/c 3rd Echelon.

Herewith War Diary for 14th
Signal Coy for month of May 1916 —

E.G.W. Harrison Major
Cmdg 14th Signal Coy

2 June 1916

XIV Division Signals

Army Form C. 2118.

WAR DIARY
or
INTELLIGENCE SUMMARY
(Erase heading not required.)

[14th SIGNAL COMPANY stamp]

Place	Date	Hour	Summary of Events and Information	Remarks and references to Appendices
WARLUS	1 May		Nothing to report.	
	4 "		41st Inf/Bde withdrawn from line & replaced by a Brigade from 5th Div. This unit took over all lines as they stood. 41st Bde H/Q established at SAVY near AUBIGNY	
	22 "		41st Bde H/Q shifted to M-St ELOI	
	27 "		" " " " ACQ	

1st June 1916.

[signature] Major
14th Signal Coy.

Army Form C. 2118.

Vol 9

WAR DIARY
or
INTELLIGENCE SUMMARY.
(Erase heading not required.)

Place	Date	Hour	Summary of Events and Information	Remarks and references to Appendices
WARLUS	1 June		Divisional H.Q in Chateau WARLUS (K 36 d 7·3 sheet 51 C NE "B"Series)	
			41st Bde H.Q in ECOIVRES (F 13 b 9·1 map 51 C NE "B" Series) attached to 17th Corps.	
	2"		42" " " Rue des Fours ARRAS	
			43" " " at DAINVILLE	
	3"		Inspection of Company horses by Corps Commander - who expressed himself very well satisfied with their condition. Stated to feel great credit on all concerned	
	4"		(7m)Lt. S.G. Anderson R.E.) RA Signals awarded Military Cross in London Gazette 2·VI·16	
			No 47242 Sergt. Sharpe R.E. 42 nd Bde Signals awarded the D.C.M " " "
			No 40209 Corp. Harris R.E. H.Q. 14 th Signals awarded the Military Medal " " "
	17 "		43 rd Bde H.Q. heavily shelled. They had to evacuate & open a new Office at 5 Rue de Watru DAINVILLE.	
	18 "		41st Bde Returned to 14 th Division	
	20/21		Right of "J" Sector taken over by 42 nd I.B.	
	21/22		43 rd Bde relieved the 15 th I.B. in J Sector.	
	22/23		41 " " " " 13 th I.B. in K "	

WAR DIARY

INTELLIGENCE SUMMARY

(Erase heading not required.)

Army Form C. 2118.

Place	Date	Hour	Summary of Events and Information	Remarks and references to Appendices
	22nd		G.O.C. XIV Div. assumed command of whole 5th Division front. Lines of 14th & 5th Signal Companies linked up at 9 A.M in accordance with attached time table.	
	27th		+2nd D.B. carried out Gas Attack, during retaliation after attack all lines held & communication was kept throughout to Companies & Battalions. The B.G.C. expressed great satisfaction with efficient way Signals of No 3 section worked under y/Lt. Colbeck- Welch. during day 153 Despatches & 330 messages were dealt with at that office.	
MARIUS	30th		No further changes - nothing to report. Total Signal Traffic at Div: H.Q for June 1916.	
			Messages sent 4423 Telephone Calls 6490	
			" Received 4370 Despatch documents 3532	
			" Transmitted 7878	
			Total 16671 Grand Total 26,693	

D.W. McNoyd
O.C. 14th Signals.

Copy No. ....

RELIEF OF 5TH DIVN BY 14TH DIVN.

The following alterations in Infantry Lines will take place between the 20th and 22nd June 1916; both dates inclusive.

Unit going in.	Unit coming out.	Nature of Line.	Rear portion of Line.	Forward portion of Line.	Joined up at.
43rd Inf. Bde	15th Inf. Bde	Telephone pair to YN. (air-line)	YN. to Wagnonlieu	FL.6 a. and b to YE.	Wagnonlieu L.21.d.7.5
- do -	- do -	- do -	FL.6 a. and b	FL.7 a. and b.	Wagnonlieu L.16.c.3.4
	95th Inf. Bde.	Telephone pair to YN.	FR.1 a and b (air-line.)	FR.1 a and b (buried.)	*Junction of Aerial and buried lines near Dainville Rly. (L.27.d.1.7 Aerial pair to YE to be cut out at same place.

Note:- The above connections to be made on morning of 21st inst at 7. A.M.
* Pole 52.

41st Inf. Bde	15th Inf. Bde	Sounder Line to YN.	YN to YE.	YE to ZO.	in YE Office. Sounder at YE to become intermediate between YN and ZO.

(This connection to be made on completion of relief of ZO by ZDC.)

Issued at:- 10.0 P.M.
Copies to:- No 1. 14th Div Staff (for information.)
2. 6th Corps Signals
3. 41st Infantry Bde Signals.
4. 43rd " " "
5. 5th Div. Signals.
6. O.C. No 1. Section.
7. File.

J.W. Barker
Major
Comdg. 14th Signal Co. R.E.

19. June 1916

14/ 14 Signals Vol 10 July

SECRET.

14th Signal Company R.E.

War Diary for July 1916.

WAR DIARY
INTELLIGENCE SUMMARY
(Erase heading not required.)

Army Form C. 2118.

Instructions regarding War Diaries and Intelligence Summaries are contained in F.S. Regs., Part II. and the Staff Manual respectively. Title pages will be prepared in manuscript.

Place	Date	Hour	Summary of Events and Information	Remarks and references to Appendices
WARLUS	1916 1 July		No change in distribution of Company	
		1.30 PM	All air lines on DAINVILLE - WARLUS road broken by shell fire. Mine exploded on centre of 41st I.B. Company lines affected, no damage to divisional lines	
	23rd	6.30 AM	42nd Bde in "H" Sector relieved 43rd I.B. in "J" Sector. 43rd Bde relieved 43rd I.B. in "J" Sector. Distribution at present as follows:-
			"J" Sector 42nd I.B. ; "J" Sector 43rd I.B. ; "K" Sector 41st I.B.	
	27th	10 PM	42nd Bde handed over "J" sector & marched to Agnez-les-Duisans	
	28th	8 PM	43rd " " " " " " " " " "	
			42nd Bde marched to GRAND RULLECOURT - WARLUZEL - GRAND RULLECOURT	
	29th		43rd " " " " OCCOCHES	
			43rd " " " GRAND RULLECOURT - WARLUZEL	
			41st " relieved by 110 Bde in K Sector & marched to AGNEZ-LES-DUISANS.	
	30th	10 AM	Division HQ closed at WARLUS at 10 AM & reopened at SUS-ST-LEGER same hour 41st Bde marched to GRAND-RULLECOURT.	

WAR DIARY
INTELLIGENCE SUMMARY.
(Erase heading not required.)

Place	Date	Hour	Summary of Events and Information	Remarks and references to Appendices
	30th	10	43rd Inf Bde marched to REMAISNIL	
	31st	9.30 AM	Div. H.Q. closed at SUS-ST-LEGER and reopened at FROHEN LE GRAND at same hour. Signal Office in Chateau. In telephonic communication with 42nd Bde and Visual to 43rd Bde	
			42nd Bde moved to FIENVILLERS	
			41st " " " OCCOCHES	
			Divisional Artillery still at WARLUS.	
			All above places shown on LENS sheet scale 1/100 000	
			Traffic for July. Messages 22156. Despatches 4862. Telephone calls 5091.	

In the field
1st August 1916.

D.W.McMahon
Major
Cmdg 14th Signals

14th Division

14th DIVISIONAL SIGNAL COMPANY

ROYAL ENGINEERS.

AUGUST 1916

Attached: Diagrams of Lines

WAR DIARY

INTELLIGENCE SUMMARY.

(Erase heading not required.)

Army Form C. 2118.

Place	Date	Hour	Summary of Events and Information	Remarks and references to Appendices
BERNAVILLE	1916 Aug 1	9.30 A.M.	Div: HQ closed at FROHEN-LE-GRAND and reopened at BERNAVILLE both at same hour (9.30 am).	Leenthel 10,000.
			41st Bde moved to GÉZAINCOURT	
			42nd " remained at FIENVILLERS	
			43rd " moved to LE MEILLARD	
			Signal Office of Division in the Mairie.	
			Telephonic communication all round.	
			43rd Bde in Visual communication with all its battalions.	
- " -	2nd		Division remained halted.	
- " -	6th		Horse Transport of Signal Coy & Forepart section marched at 11 AM and Latter for night at RAINNEVILLE	
BUIRE-SUR-L'ANCRE	7th		Transport marched at 8 AM and arrived new HQ at 1 P.M. Div HQ closed down at BERNAVILLE at 12 noon and reopen new position at BUIRE-SUR-L'ANCRE same hour.	
- " -	8th		Div HQ at BUIRE 42nd Bde BUIRE 43rd Bde North of DERNANCOURT 41st Bde DERNANCOURT.	

WAR DIARY or INTELLIGENCE SUMMARY

Army Form C. 2118.

Place	Date	Hour	Summary of Events and Information	Remarks and references to Appendices
BUIRE	9th		Division remained halted.	
	12th		43rd Bde took over portion of front line from 52nd I.B.	
			42nd " Moved up into reserve at FRICOURT in relief of 51st Bde	
	13th	8:30 AM	41st Bde took over portion of front line from 50th I.B. Sergt Thompson wounded	
		10 AM	Div HQ closed at BUIRE-sur-L'ANCRE and reopened at BELLEVUE FARM (F.S.C central) same time in relief of 17th Division.	
ALBERT	14th		No change.	
	15th	3:30 AM	Started digging trench for line to DELVILLE WOOD	
	16th	3:30 AM	Continued trench	
	17th	3:30 AM	" "	
	18th	9:45 PM	41st and 43rd Bdes carried out attack capturing orchard/trench/portion of Delville Wood. Signal Coy Casualties: 1 officer wounded (at duty) 1 O.R. killed 2 wounded. All lines worked well. Lines in Communication Trenches went. Burne. line held.	
	19th	3:30 AM	Strengthened lines	
	20-22nd		Continued forward work. 2nd Lieut Mureton wounded.	

WAR DIARY
or
INTELLIGENCE SUMMARY.

Army Form C. 2118.

Place	Date	Hour	Summary of Events and Information	Remarks and references to Appendices
ALBERT (Bellevue Farm)	23rd	3.30 AM	Work continued.	
	24th	5.45 PM	Attack by 42nd & 41st Bdes commenced, in conjunction with general offensive.	
			Advanced HdQrs at S.28.a.0.4 and S.22.d.0.3	
			41st I.B. failed to reach objective	
			42nd I.B. made good progress	
	25th		42nd I.B. captured whole of DELVILLE WOOD.	
			All lines held & communication worked without a break.	
	26th		42nd I.B. relieved by 22nd I.B. 42nd became Divisional Reserve.	
	27th		41st I.B. relieved by 43rd I.B.	
			43rd I.B. HQ at Pommiers Redoubt. One man wounded.	
			41st Bde relieved to DERNANCOURT	
			41st Bde railed to AIRAINES	
	30th		42nd - moved to DERNANCOURT.	
	31st		Div HQ closed down at BELLE VUE FARM and reopened at BELLOY ST LEONARD at 12 Noon.	
			Diagrams of lines taken over were in line LONGUEVAL - DELVILLE WOOD attached hereto.	

J.W. McGregor
Capt. 14th Signals

2.9.16

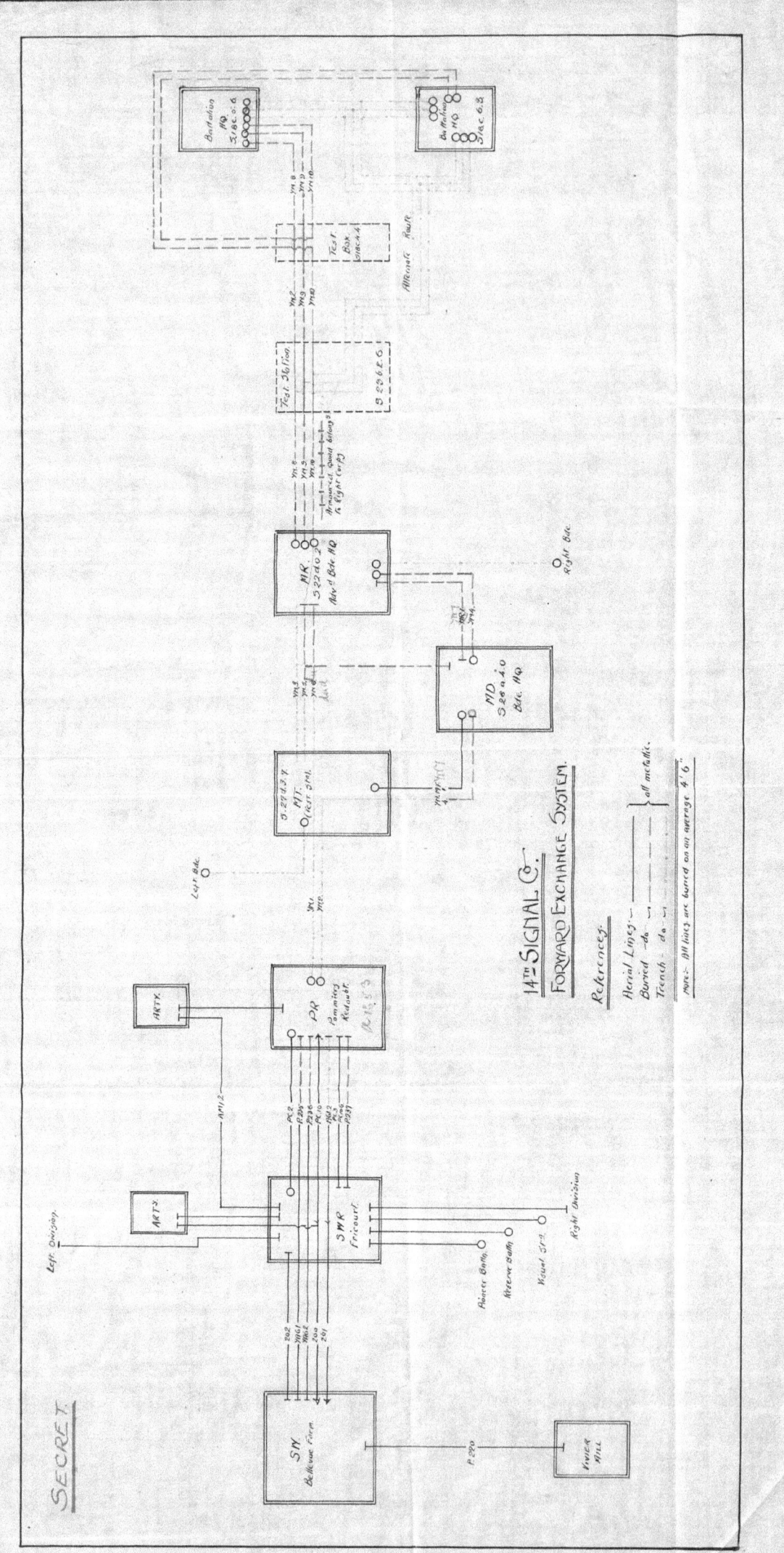

14th SIGNAL C. ROUTE MAP.

Scale 1:20,000.

Reference.

Aerial Lines shown in Black.
Buried   do   do   do   Red.
French   do   do   do   Green.

C.H. Barker Major.
Comdg 14th Signal Co R.E.

August 1916.

Vol 12

<u>Confidential</u>

War Diary
of
14th Signal Co R.E.

From 1.9.16. To 30.9.16.
(Volume 16.)

WAR DIARY or INTELLIGENCE SUMMARY

Army Form C. 2118.

Place	Date	Hour	Summary of Events and Information	Remarks and references to Appendices
FRICOURT	17th	10 AM	Handed over to 21st Division	
BUIRE			Div HQ established at BUIRE sur l'ANCRE	
			All Brigades out of line.	
	21st		Transport left for le CAUROY.	
	22nd	Mdn	Div HQ closed at BUIRE and reopened at le CAUROY halting for night at TALMAS	Ammunt Iron Shot 1/100,000
le CAUROY			BRIGADES located as follows	
			41st J.B. LUCHEUX	
			42nd J.B. GRAND RULLECOURT	
			43rd J.B. SUS ST LEGER	
GOUY	26th	10 AM	Div HQ closed at le CAUROY and reopened at GOUY	
WARLUS	28 PAM		Div HQ closed at GOUY and reopened at WARLUS	
			41st J.B. holding "F" Sector HQ at DAINVILLE	
			42nd JB " "G" " ARRAS	
			43rd JB " "H" " "	
			Diagram of lines for fighting on the SOMME and also separate report marked A.V.S respectively attached hereto.	

EgeBelhman
Cml 14 Signals.

Army Form C. 2118.

WAR DIARY
or
INTELLIGENCE SUMMARY.
(Erase heading not required.)

Instructions regarding War Diaries and Intelligence Summaries are contained in F.S. Regs., Part II. and the Staff Manual respectively. Title pages will be prepared in manuscript.

Place	Date	Hour	Summary of Events and Information	Remarks and references to Appendices
BELLOY ST LEONARD	1 Sept	Noon	Office opened for Division in Chateau. Division at rest. 41st Inf Bde — HEUCOURT 42nd " — AVESNES CHAUSSEY 43rd " — HORNOY	Abbeville Map. 1 / 100,000.
	10 "	11 AM	Horse Transport and men with bicycles left for AILLY sur SOMME to billet en route for BUIRE sur L'ANCRE	
BUIRE	11 "	12 noon	Division H.Q. closed down at BELLOY and reopened at BUIRE	
FRICOURT	12 "	"	Division H.Q. moved to FRICOURT CHATEAU. Signal office established in German dug-out.	
	13 "	8.30 am	G.O.C. took over line with 41st Bde at MONTAUBAN S28a.4.0. 42nd " " FRICOURT CAMP 43rd " " DERNANCOURT	
			41st Bde moved to advanced H.Q. at S23a.9.3 42nd " " " MONTAUBAN S28a 4.0. 43rd " " " FRICOURT CAMP Much work put in digging trench for cable to Advanced Battn HQ S12dg.1	

Army Form C. 2118.

WAR DIARY
or
INTELLIGENCE SUMMARY.
(Erase heading not required.)

Instructions regarding War Diaries and Intelligence Summaries are contained in F. S. Regs., Part II. and the Staff Manual respectively. Title pages will be prepared in manuscript.

Place	Date	Hour	Summary of Events and Information	Remarks and references to Appendices
FRICOURT	Sept. 15	A.M. 6.30	41st Bde attack in first objective	Maps:— LONGUEVAL Edition 2E 5.7 SW 3 / 10,000
		6.20	General attack along whole line	
			Diagram of lines & plan attached hereto. Lines as far as Bazar Wd held – and also up S10 C 6.3. From there onwards through DELVILLE WOOD, lines were cut as fast as laid. 41st Bde Section attempted flag line following infantry advance from S12 d 5.9 to T 7 6.68 but these lines were broken as fast as laid.	
		10 AM	Visual party of 1 NCO & 6 OR sent to N.E. corner of DELVILLE WOOD to endeavour to keep touch with advancing troops. Barrage started as they were crossing Wood, wounding 4 OR. The NCO & OR proceed to their position and opened Visual Station at S.12 d 5.4.9	
		7.30 PM	Both M0 in S 10 C 6.3 connected by wire to Visual Station S12 d 5.4.9, but line out of use	
	16th	5.15 AM	Wireless Station established at S12 d 5.5. to work in conjunction with the Visual & thus save runners having to cross Barrage area in Delville Wood. Was not actually required as telephone line held.	

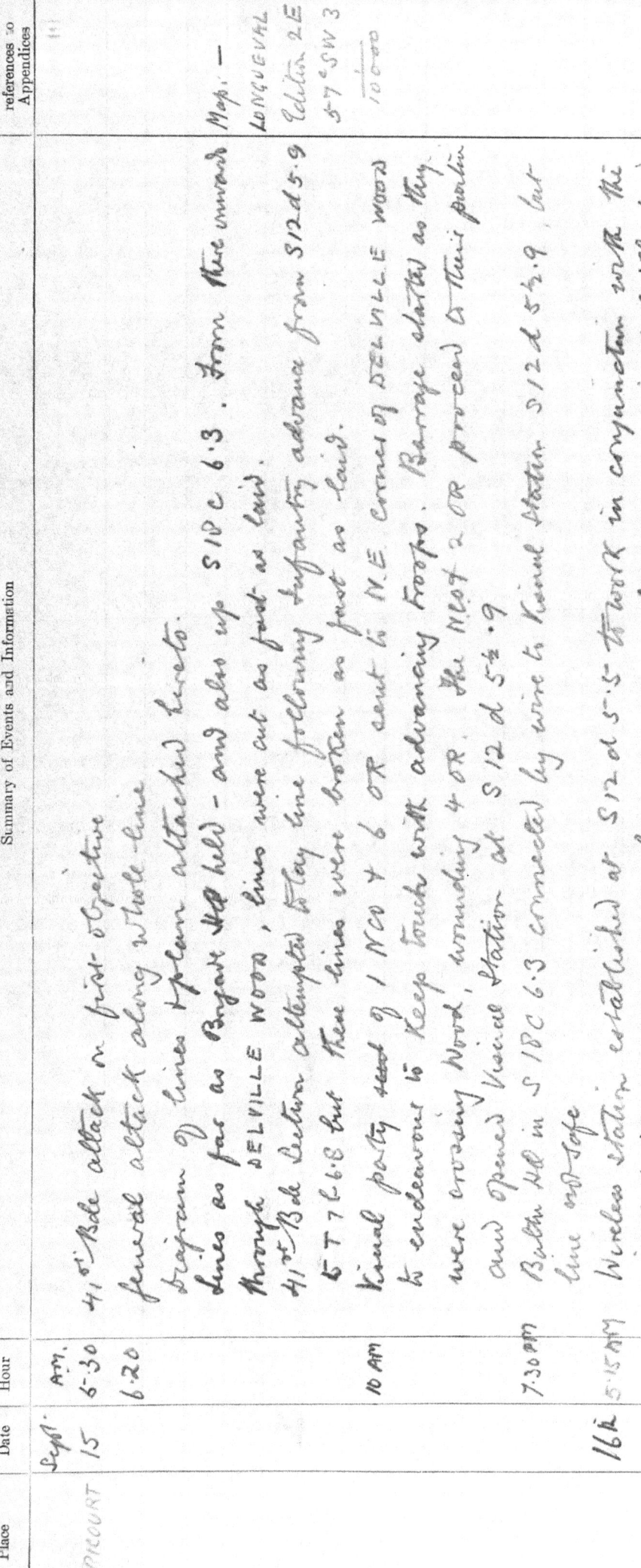

REPORT on SIGNAL WORK DURING OPERATIONS

13th to 17th September 1916 (both inclusive).

13th Sept.

41st Infantry Brigade H.Q. were established at MONTAUBAN on the morning of 13th inst. with two battalion H.Qs. in DELVILLE WOOD, other two Battalions in support.

An Advanced H.Q. had been constructed at S 23 a 9.3 in YORK TRENCH, but was not in telegraphic communication, though Corps Signals were building a buried route. During 13th and morning of 14th, I had working parties of King's Liverpools digging a trench for burying lines from an old buried route I constructed for the attack on 24th August. They were also employed in strengthening and repairing lines to Battalion H.Q. at Cable Head (S 18 c 6.3)

14th Sept.

These lines were completed on morning of 14th. Advanced Brigade H.Q. was thus connected up with Div.H.Q. at FRICOURT, and with their Battalions in DELVILLE WOOD, and ready for occupation by 9 a.m.

A party from 41st Brigade Signals spent the day (14th) in laying armoured cable from Battalion H.Q. at Cable Head (S 18 c 6.3) to position selected for Advanced Battalion H.Q. in GREEN STREET (S 12 d 5½.9). The construction of this line was somewhat delayed on account of some uncertainty as to where Battalion H.Q. were going to be. It was however completed and in working order by 1.0 a.m. on 15th inst., but was broken by two direct hits about 5 a.m. It was quickly put through again by linemen and held up till 9.30 a.m. when DELVILLE WOOD was heavily barraged.

The Advanced Battalion H.Q. was not ready for occupation till 4.30 a.m. on the morning of attack.

41st Brigade H.Q. moved from MONTAUBAN to advanced Brigade H.Q. at 2 p.m. on 14th inst. They were then in touch with all their units.

15th Sept.

The Corps Cable was not ready for use till 5.20 a.m. on morning of attack, owing I believe to Cable trench being used by Infantry. When attack started, lines were working well and held throughout with slight interruptions as far as Battalion H.Q. cable head. The heavy shelling broke line through DELVILLE WOOD about 9.30 a.m. which through lack of time had had to be put in a communication trench. From the commencement of the attack at 5.30 a.m. till it was broken, the line was fully occupied by reports and F.O.O. messages. The last message to be sent was one from 7th K.R.R.C. reporting occupation of the blue line.

Linemen were out after that all the time repairing it, but as fast as it was repaired it was broken. But line as far as old Battalion H.Q. at S 18 c 6.3 held.

Communication after 9.30 a.m. between Battalion H.Q. and the firing line was therefore maintained by

(a). Pigeons (separate report attached)

(b). Runners to S 18 c 6.3, thence telegraph.

(c). Visual.

(d). Aeroplane.

Sgt. THOMPSON and a lineman of 41st Brigade Signals endeavoured to follow Battalions up - but as quick as the line was laid it was broken by shell fire. At 10.30 a.m. as previously arranged, a party of Visual signallers went to open Central Visual Station at S 12 d 5½.9. As they were crossing the barrage area a shell burst, burying 8 out of 10 of them. Corporal Roberts and L/Cpl. MURDOCK of the King's Liverpools (two of the signallers) and Pioneer Copp extricated themselves. The remainder of the party was dug-out by men from 8th Rifle Bde., but were too badly injured to proceed. A good deal of equipment was lost. I think great credit is due to Corporal Roberts in collecting what gear he could and pushing on at once with Corporal MURDOCK. The station was established and signals exchanged with 8th K.R.R.C. But the latter did not attempt to send any messages. Battalions of 41st Brigade were notified by their Brigade Major in his B.M.101 of the locality of this station, but I do not think they realised its possibilities, and no battalions of this Brigade used this invaluable means of communication, but stuck to runners. This made receipt of reports from the front much slower. I believe that no battalions used their signal officer as such - which is a pity.

Owing to the impossibility of maintaining a line through DELVILLE WOOD, I decided to lay a line round it, and this was done. I also moved a wireless set to S 12 d 4.9 with receiving set at Advanced Brigade H.Q. This arrangement gave me a good visual station which could keep in touch with Infantry units, a telephone line back to Brigade, and wireless, should the telephone line break. As a matter of fact, the telephone held, and so wireless was not required.

16th Sept.

All units of the 43rd Brigade were informed of whereabouts of visual station. Throughout the fighting messages came through very quickly and well to visual station, and thence were telephoned to Advanced Brigade H.Q. This line gave little trouble, any breaks being quickly repaired by lineman. The Battalions of this Brigade were slow in taking advantage of this means of communication. The Central station at GREEN trench was ready for work when the Battalions went forward and the Battalion signal officer of the Somerset L.I. was personally taken to it on the evening of the 15th.

It was not till 9 a.m. on the 16th that messages were coming in, and from then onwards a lot of work was got through.

I attach a diagram of lines, and also a report on pigeon messages.

I do not think all battalions quite realise the possibilities of Visual during an offensive, as many more reports could have been received and much time saved in their transmission if they had used this means. The country and weather were most favourable for this method of communication.

I would suggest that when future offensive operations are in contemplation, the O.C. Brigade Signal Sections should be present at the conference of Commanding officers held by the Brigadier. I think better arrangements could have been made if this had been done.

The two battalions of the 43rd Brigade supplied with pigeons made no use of them.

Runners.

The work done by Battalion runners on both days was beyond praise. I am endeavouring to find out men who especially distinguished themselves, but where all did so well, this is a difficult matter.

I am drawing up scheme for their training based on experiences gained during the recent fighting, which I propose submitting to you in a few days.

The total number of messages and despatches dealt with at Divisional H.Q. on 15th was 1017. Many of the messages from Corps were exceptionally long. On 16th a total of 960 were dealt with. The above do not include telephone calls.

23/9/1916

Major,
Cmdng. 14th Signal Coy. R.E.

"A"

14th SIGNAL Cᵒ.
Route Map.

Scale 1:20000

Reference:—
Aerial Lines ————
Buried do. —————
Trench do. ·········
Poled and Trenched. —·—·—

Arthur du Bou—
Capt. RE.
for O.C. 14th Signal Cᵒ. RE.
September 1916.

REPORT ON CARRIER PIGEON SERVICE

during attack on 15th and 16th

September, 1916.

Birds were supplied to Battalions as follows :-

41st Inf. Bde. 4 pairs to 8th K.R.R.C.
                4   "   " 8th Rif. Bde.
                2   "   " 7th K.R.R.C.
                2   "   " 7th Rif. Bde.

42nd Inf. Bde. No birds available.

43rd Inf. Bde. 2 pairs to 10th Durham L.I.
                2   "   " 6th Somerset L.I.

The following table shows the messages carried by each pair, the time taken in flight and in Telegraphic transmission from the Loft.

Messages. From	Message No.	Birds despatched at	Received at Loft at	Received at Divn.	Received by addressee.	Remarks.	
8 R.B.	A.1	7.30am	8.2	8.3	8.22		15th
8 R.B.	A.2	10.2am	10.38*	10.36	10.45	* Wrongly timed. Addressed to 8 R.B.	"
8 K.R.R	A.3	7.55am	8.29	8.33	8.35		"
8 K.R.R	A.4	12.45pm	1.28				"
7 K.R.R	A.5	8.40am	9.0	9.10	9.12		"
7 K.R.R	A.6	10.35am	10.38	10.38	10.38		"
7 K.R.R	A.7	6.40am	6.50			Birds had to be released (48 hours being up) Sent on 16th.	
7 R.B.	A.8	9.28am	9.50	9.54	9.58		15th

The form of communication appears to have been invaluable.

The birds issued to two battalions of the 43rd Inf. Bde. for work on 16th were not pitched. This may be accounted for by the fact that they were able to keep touch with Bde. H.Q. by visual. The following points require further attention.
    There should always be two pigeon men at each Battalion H.Q.
    These men must not be runners or signallers.
    All Officers and N.C.Os. should be shown how to fix messages in carrier, also how birds should be pitched.

                                            Major,
                              Comdg. 14th Signal Coy. R.E.

23rd September, 1916.

Confidential

War Diary
of
14th Signal Co RE

1st Oct — 31st 1916.

Volume 17

Army Form C. 2118.

WAR DIARY
or
INTELLIGENCE SUMMARY.
(Erase heading not required.)

Place	Date	Hour	Summary of Events and Information	Remarks and references to Appendices
WARLUS	Oct 1-11	—	No change in position of Division. Brigade Headquarters. No alteration in arrangements already in force.	
"	12	—	Captain Grundy R.E. arrived to take over command of Company.	
"	13.	—	Major Barker D.S.O. left the Signal Company to join A. Corps Signal Company.	
"	14-26	—	Preparations being made to move 42nd Brigade Headquarters at DAINVILLE to the Citadel at ARRAS. Wire conveyed in burying 4 pairs of cables from the Citadel to a test station (near ACHICOURT.) on the existing system of lines from Brigade Headquarters to Battalion.	
"	27	10 a.m.	Command of sector taken over by the 12th Division, to whom the existing system of lines was handed over. (Copy of diagram of existing system of lines & communication to Brigades attached.) 14th Division Headquarters opened in communication with 12th Division Headquarters.	
LE CAUROY	"	—	BEAUFORT rest area at LE CAUROY where Signal Office was established, with telephonic communication to Brigades at GRAND RULLECOURT (41st Brigade) LIENCOURT (42nd Brigade) and MANIN (43rd Brigade). This communication was established by using	

WAR DIARY
or
INTELLIGENCE SUMMARY.

(Erase heading not required.)

Army Form C. 2118.

Place	Date	Hour	Summary of Events and Information	Remarks and references to Appendices
LE CAUROY	Oct 27th Cont'd	—	Existing Corps lines.	
	28.	—	2nd Lieut MacAleese joined Signal Company as supernumary Officer from 3rd Army.	
	29.	—	43rd Brigade moved to AMBRINES. Telephonic Communication established with Division on existing Corps lines working through AVESNES Exchange.	

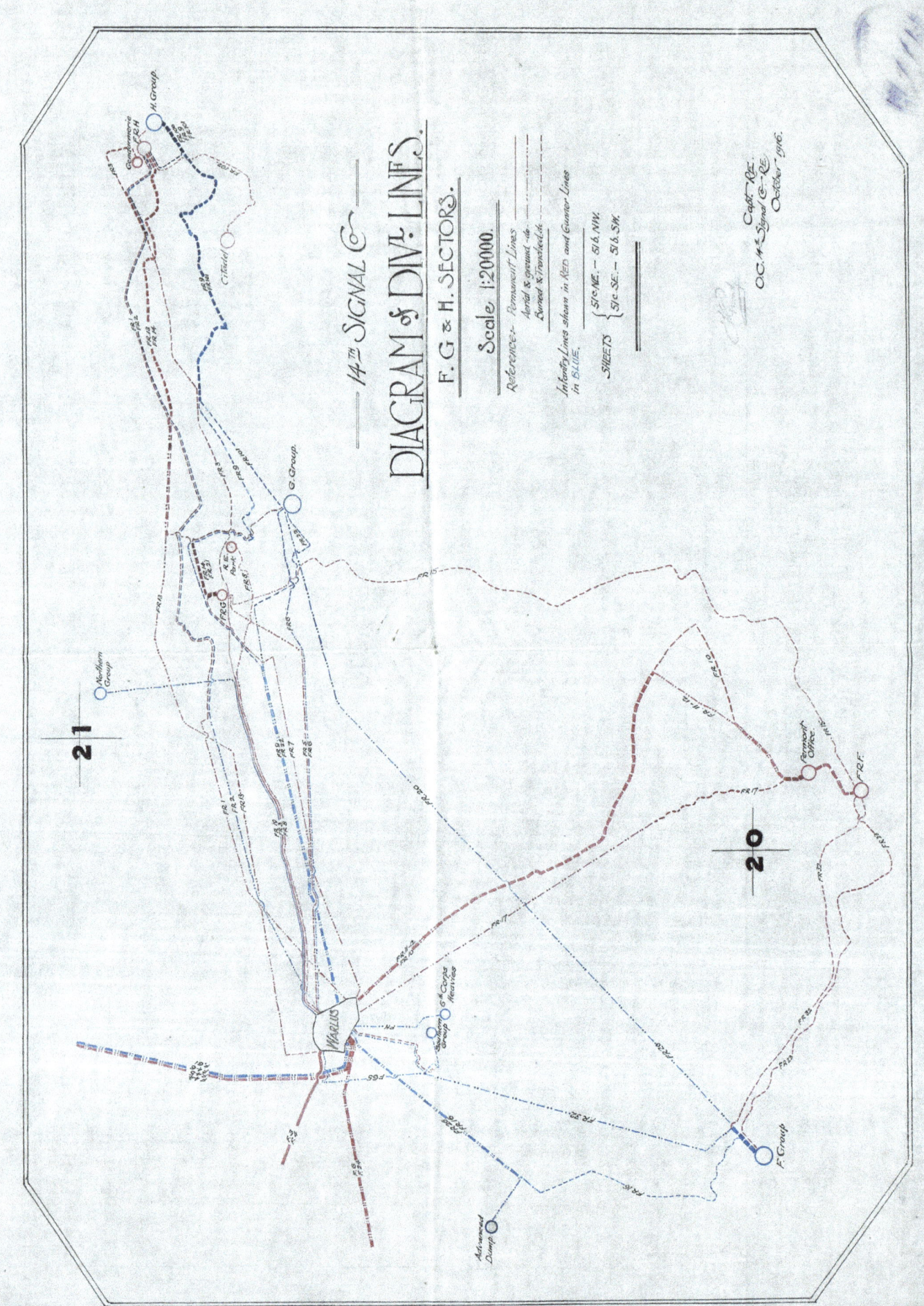

Vol/4

<u>Confidential.</u>

War Diary

of the

14th Signal Co R.E.

From Nov 1st — 30th 1916.

(Volume 18).

Army Form C. 2118.

WAR DIARY
or
INTELLIGENCE SUMMARY.
(Erase heading not required.)

Instructions regarding War Diaries and Intelligence Summaries are contained in F.S. Regs., Part II. and the Staff Manual respectively. Title pages will be prepared in manuscript.

Place	Date	Hour	Summary of Events and Information	Remarks and references to Appendices
	1-30			
	23rd		Headquarters and No 1 Section at LE CAUROY. No. 3 Section (42nd Bde) moved to GOUY. Communication established by telephone through 6th Corps.	
	10th		Sub-Office established at IVERGNY, connected by telephone, to 41st Brigade, for facilitating delivery of various units in the vicinity.	
			The Signal Company has been engaged during the month in training, particularly in mounted work, and in making improvements to billets and stables.	

Grundy Capt. RE.
OC 14th Divisional Signal Co.

Vol 15

<u>Confidential</u>

War Diary
of the
14th Signal Company R.E.
From 1st Dec to 31st Dec 1916.

(Volume 19)

Army Form C. 2118.

WAR DIARY
or
INTELLIGENCE SUMMARY.
(Erase heading not required.)

Instructions regarding War Diaries and Intelligence Summaries are contained in F. S. Regs., Part II. and the Staff Manual respectively. Title pages will be prepared in manuscript.

Place	Date	Hour	Summary of Events and Information	Remarks and references to Appendices
LE CAUROY	1/6/18		Headquarters at LE CAUROY, with telephonic & telegraphic communication to the VI Corps at NOYELLE VION, and telephonic communication to each Brigade.	
	19		Personnel engaged in training and improving rest billets. Company moved to WARLUS, relieving the 12th Divisional Signal Company, in sectors F, G, and H. Men and communications exactly as handed over to the 12th Signal Company on October 27th.	
	20-31		Communications as follows:- Telephone and sounder to each Brigade - 41st at BRETENCOURT, 42nd at DAINVILLE, 43rd at ARRAS. The 12th Divisional Artillery being in the area, the 12th Signal Company left one Officer and 6 men to run the Artillery lines, which consist mainly of a telephone and buzzer to each Brigade.	
	28		The wireless station in H Sector moved from position near ACHICOURT to RONVILLE, G 34 b 3.3 (sheet 51bNW), and communication established with directing station at WARLUS.	

H Kennedy Capt RE
OC 14th Divisional Signal Co.

1577 Wt. W10791/1773 500,000 1/15 D. D. & L. A.D.S.S./Forms/C. 2118.

Vol 16

Confidential.

War Diary.
of the
14th Signal Company R.E.

From   1 - 31 January 1917.

(Volume 20.)

WAR DIARY
or
INTELLIGENCE SUMMARY.

(Erase heading not required.)

Army Form C. 2118.

Instructions regarding War Diaries and Intelligence Summaries are contained in F. S. Regs., Part II. and the Staff Manual respectively. Title pages will be prepared in manuscript.

Place	Date	Hour	Summary of Events and Information	Remarks and references to Appendices
	Jan 1917			
	8th		Positions of Divisional Headquarters and Brigade Headquarters remained the same as before, no change in existing communications being made.	
	8th		The 14th Division was transferred from 6th Corps to 7th Corps, but there being no change in divisional area, no change was required in the system of lines within the Division. New 6 foot deep buried scheme begun. During the month 1½ miles of bury was dug from the Citadel as far as L.29.a.8.2 (Sheet 51c). Also from G.32.b.3.1 to G.33.a.5.2. The digging party, averaging 200 daily, was provided by 17th. Lancashire Fusiliers under arrangements of 6th Corps.	
	14th		2/7th J.S. Kilpatrick, 10th A.& S.H., joined the Company on one month's probation. Classes of instruction for Artillery and Battalion Signallers (about 30 of each) were held during the month under divisional arrangements.	

H Hammond Capt RE
OC 14th Signal Co.
31 January 1917.

Confidential.

War Diary
of the
14th Signal Company R.E.

From 1st Feby 1917 — 28th Feby 1917.

(Volume ~~21~~)

Army Form C. 2118.

WAR DIARY
or
INTELLIGENCE SUMMARY.
(Erase heading not required.)

Instructions regarding War Diaries and Intelligence Summaries are contained in F. S. Regs., Part II. and the Staff Manual respectively. Title pages will be prepared in manuscript.

Place	Date	Hour	Summary of Events and Information	Remarks and references to Appendices
WARLUS	3/2/17		41st Bde relieved in F Sector by 127 Brigade. Opened office in GRAND RULLECOURT. Telephonic communication. Brigade See section personnel established schools for battalion signallers	
do	6/2/17		42nd Bde relieved in G Sector by 89th Brigade and 21st Bde 6th of 30th Division. Ex same	
do	7/2/17		42nd Bde relieved 43rd Bde in left half of M Sector H.Q. in Amas 42nd Bde relieved 43rd Bde in left half of M Sector Cable burying on Corps System began. One party of 500 men detailed from 42nd Brigade for work on Corps System under Supervision of Divisional Signals. One party of 300 men (150 from 42nd Bde and 150 from 43rd Bde) detailed for Divisional work under Divisional Signal Company. Carrier action of buried system forward.	
do	7/2/17 to 28/2/17			
do	27/2/17		Divisional Signal School opened at GRAND RULLECOURT in conjunction with Divisional Depot Battalion.	
	27/2/17			

1577 Wt.W10791/1773 500,000 1/15 D.D.&L. A.D.S.S./Forms/C. 2118.

A. Underh Capt R.E.
for O.C. 14th S. Co.

WAR DIARY

INTELLIGENCE SUMMARY

Army Form C. 2118.

Page	Date	Hour	Summary of Events and Information	Remarks and references to Appendices
WARLUS	1-3-17		During the month the buried cable scheme was completed in the Divisional Area preparatory for offensive action. All routes were buried in tunnels or seven foot deep in tunnels or severe. A class for Battalion signallers was started at the beginning of the month at the Divisional School at GRAND RULLECOURT. The class numbered 56, the instruction being carried out by an officer and 6 instructors from the Signal Company. The instruction lasted one month and consisted chiefly of visual signalling. On the 16th the 41st Infy Brigade moved from GRAND RULLECOURT to GOUY. Communication by telegraphs and telephone was established via the Corps. On the 18th, owing to the retirement of the German line, a Battalion of the 43rd Infy Brigade moved to the BRICKFIELDS at M5a1-1 sheet 51C. Communication was established by wire, visual and wireless. German buried cables were also brought into use.	

Army Form C. 2118.

WAR DIARY
INTELLIGENCE SUMMARY.
(Erase heading not required.)

Instructions regarding War Diaries and Intelligence Summaries are contained in F. S. Regs., Part II. and the Staff Manual respectively. Title pages will be prepared in manuscript.

Place	Date	Hour	Summary of Events and Information	Remarks and references to Appendices
			These were found to be buried from 10 to 12 foot deep and were out forwards of the British front line. An IT was established in Dugout at M5b 4.9 and connected to forward sections of German buried cables, but no results were obtained. On the 22nd, the 41st Inf Brigade moved from GOUY to ARRAS and relieved the 42nd and 43rd Inf Brigades in the front line. The 43rd Inf Brigade remained at their Headquarters in ARRAS and the 42nd Inf Brigade Headquarters were established at BERNEVILLE. Direct telegraph and telephone communication was maintained with all Brigades. The extension of buried routes was carried forward to the German lines as far as M5 b 6.9 in the left sector, and M5a 1.1 in the right sector. Divisional Headquarters remained at WARLUS.	

[Signature]
Capt R.E.
OC 14th Signal Co R.E.

[Stamp: 14th SIGNAL COMPANY R.E.]

Confidential.

War Diary
of the
14th Signal Company R.E.
from 1st to 30th April 1917.

(Volume 23.)

A.G's Office at the Base.

        Herewith War Diary of the 14th Divisional
Signal Coy R.E. for the month of April, 1917.
        Please acknowledge receipt.

                        Major General,
24/5/17.   Commanding 14th (Light) Division.

WAR DIARY or INTELLIGENCE SUMMARY

(Erase heading not required.)

Place	Date	Hour	Summary of Events and Information	Remarks and references to Appendices
	1/68		Final preparations for communications for attack on Telegraph Hill. Lines on the buried routes were tested out and joined up to give required circuits. Forward Artillery Exchange established in Churchwell Cave.	
	2.		41st Brigade relieved by 42nd on left and 43rd on right. 42nd HdQrs at Factory G.35.a.0.7, 43rd Brigade in Kehra Trench G.34.d.8.8, and 41st Bde in caves.	
	3.		All arrangements for communications were complete by evening of 8th. Attached diagram No.1 shows the Available communications for Infantry and Artillery of the Division. "14th Division Signal Communications for the Offensive" Attached gives all the arrangements made for utilizing the Auxiliary means of Communication, and for establishing communication after capture of objective. On the evening of the 6th every pair of wires had been laid out in GINGER STREET, turned into the pice plinth, as far as BATTERY TRENCH, at M.12.d.0.4. Five of these pairs were connected on to and L RFA Brigade, to be extended for use of FOO's after capture of 1st Objective, and the wire allotted to the Infantry for extending to Forward Brigade Station to be established at M.12.d.8.4.	
	9		Attack launched, and communications established as arranged. Brigade Headquarters were moved, 42nd to M.5.b.6.9, and 43rd to M.5.d.7.4, and renamed	

WAR DIARY
INTELLIGENCE SUMMARY

Army Form C. 2118.

Place	Date	Hour	Summary of Events and Information	Remarks and references to Appendices
	10.		on telephonic and telegraphic communication with division; 1st Brigade where the 42nd & 43rd Headquarters being established at N7d4.0. A forward Brigade Post was chosen, and communication established as shown in Diagram No 2. Being at the length of line from Division to Brigade; Linesmens Posts were established at several points along the line. Besides the test dugouts on the buried cable system, linesmen were stationed at LONEN SCHANZE, N5d7.4, and ZZ (M12d 8.9). Shelling was not very heavy, and lines were not cut, although from BT (M12d 0.9) they were laid over the ground. (attached) "Notes on Communications during the Offensive 9-13th April 1917" give a short resumé of communication.	
	12 & 13		The Division was relieved by 50th Div. 14th Div. HdQrs remained at WARLUS, and the 3 Brigades moved by stages into rest area. During the moves communication was maintained with them by Despatch Rider only. The Division came under orders of 18th Corps, with whom communication by telephone and telegraph superimposed, was obtained.	

WAR DIARY or INTELLIGENCE SUMMARY

Army Form C. 2118.

Place	Date	Hour	Summary of Events and Information	Remarks and references to Appendices
	16.		By this date Brigades were settled in, viz. 42nd at LIENCOURT, 43rd at SVS ST LEGER. Communication was mostly by Despatch Rider, lines not being available in the wet air.	
	24.		Divisional Headquarters moved to BAILLEULMONT, communication obtained with the Corps. Brigades moved by stages to same area, but communication only obtained by Despatch Rider.	
	26		14th Division relieved 30th Division, with Headquarters at ARRAS, and Advanced Headquarters at N7d 4.0. 42nd Brigade took over the line with Headquarters at N15d 4.3. Communication was very sketchy, particularly in the case of the Artillery, who had 5 groups. A poled cable, of 4 pairs was at once started from Divisional Headquarters to 42nd Headquarters. This was extended to N22c.7.6. at which point a forward artillery exchange was established, with 3 telephone pairs and 1 telegraph back to CRA, and a pair to each Artillery Brigade.	
	28		41st Brigade moved into the line, taking over the night of the relief, with Headquarters at N22d 4.7. The poled cable from N22c.7.6 was extended to this point, and also a 2 pair alloudine poled cable built about 100 yds away and parallel to the 4 pair route. Each Brigade had one Battalion in the line, both Headquarters being in a forming up points in STAG TRENCH at O19a.2.3. An armoured cable was	

WAR DIARY
or
INTELLIGENCE SUMMARY.
(Erase heading not required.)

Army Form C. 2118.

Instructions regarding War Diaries and Intelligence Summaries are contained in F.S. Regs., Part II. and the Staff Manual respectively. Title pages will be prepared in manuscript.

Place	Date	Hour	Summary of Events and Information	Remarks and references to Appendices
			Laid from each Brigade to this point, with a cable between Brigades. Connection to both flank Brigades and Division was also established by telephone. Rear Headquarters in Arras were in telephonic and telegraphic communication with Advanced Headquarters and with 9th Corps. All administration departments were in the City and connected to the rear exchange.	

[Signature]
O.C. 14th Signal Co. R.E.

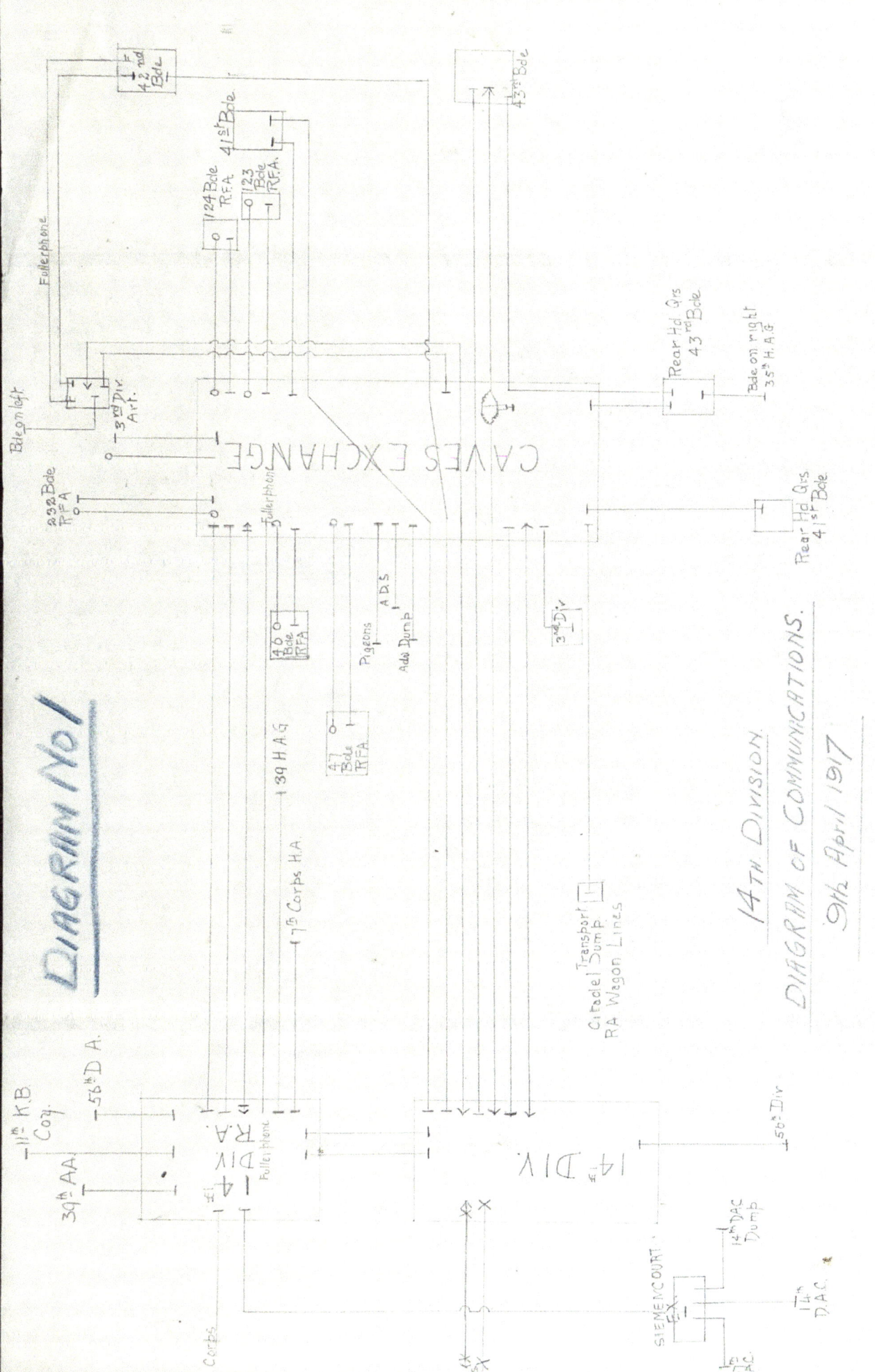

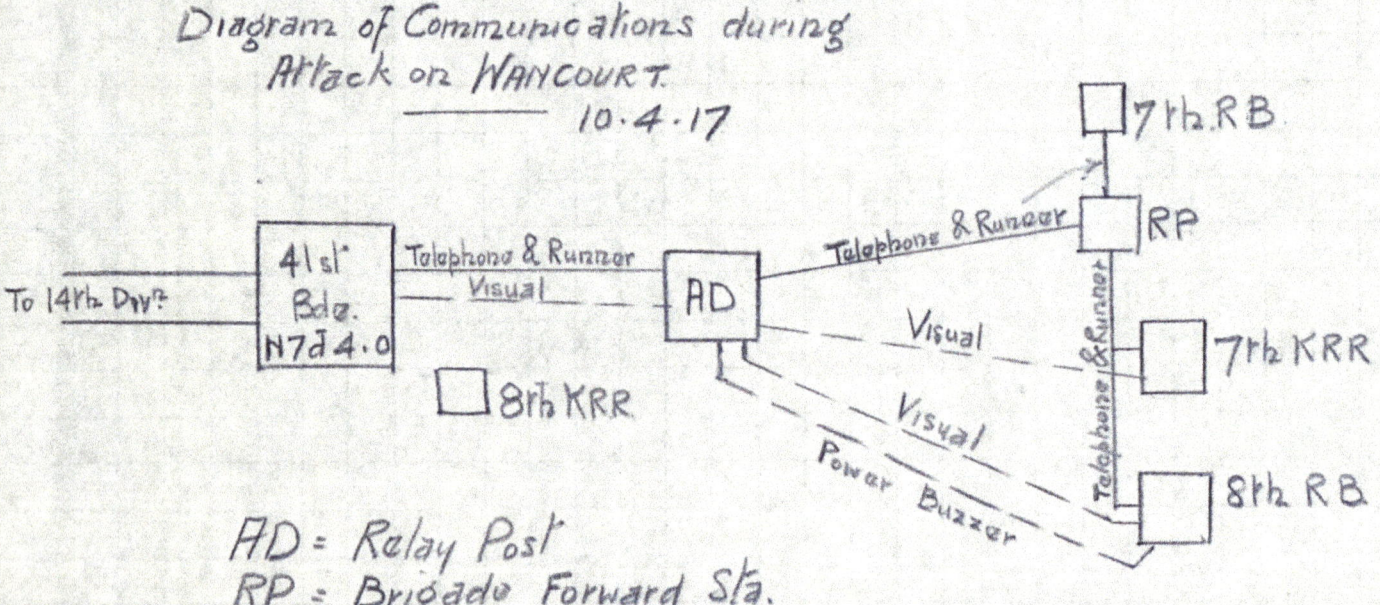

14th DIVISION.

NOTES ON COMMUNICATIONS DURING THE OFFENSIVE 9th - 13th APRIL 1917.

Telephone and Telegraph.

Telephonic and Telegraphic communication was established as arranged, as far as Brigade Command Posts.

Advanced Signal Stations were established by each Brigade connected by Telephone to Brigade Command Post, and to which Battalions in most cases ran a Telephone line.

There was very little shelling, and wires were not cut except at the Advanced Signal Station of the Left Brigade during the early stages of the attack.

An average of 1000 messages per day were transmitted by Telegraph at the Divisional Signal Office alone.

Visual.

Visual communication from the Brigade Command Post to the back receiving station was established at ZERO, but was not required, as the lines were not cut.

Brigades established Visual communication from Command Posts to Advanced Signal Stations, and this was used extensively for sending messages, the Telephone line being much used for speaking.

Visual was also established, where possible, between Advanced Signal Stations and Battalions.

Communications forwards of Battalions.

The available means of communication forwards of Battalions do not appear to have been established in many cases where they could have been utilised.

(2)

This I attribute to the want of experience on the part of the Battalion Signal Officers.

Pigeons.

Supplies of Pigeons were available throughout the battle, but were not very much used.

Nine Operation messages were sent by this means.

The Pigeons took an average time of 20 minutes to fly back to the loft, and the messages an average time of 30 minutes from the loft to the Brigade.

The latter time is too long, and efforts will be made to cut this down in future operations.

Wireless.

As soon as the Blue line was captured the 2 Wireless stations were set up at their respective Advanced Signal Stations and communication established with the Corps Directing Station.

When the Brown line was captured the Wireless Station on the right moved up to the new Brigade Head Quarters, but failed to get into touch with the Directing Station. This was due to the set having been wrongly joined up, and after being remedied, communication was established.

As Telephone communication remained intact, Wireless was not used for messages, except in one case. This message took $1\frac{1}{2}$ hours to reach the Divisional Signal Office from the Corps Station.

Amplifier and Power Buzzer.

(1) As previously arranged the Amplifier was installed at ZERO in Lowen Schanze.

One Power Buzzer went forward with a Battalion of each of the attacking Brigades.

In the case of the Left Brigade, the man carrying the

accumulator fell over, and the acid was upset, thus rendering the Buzzer useless.

No signals were received from the 43rd Brigade, and the Officer in charge of the Amplifier (Lieut Stock, 6th Som. L.I.) went out to see the Buzzer, and found that the earths had not been connected up. When this was corrected, signals were received by the Amplifier (distance about 1500 yards).

(2) For the advance from the Blue to the Brown line the Amplifier moved to the Battalion Head Quarters of the 6th Somerset Light Infantry, but had only a shell hole in which to work.

No signals were received, and on investigation Lieut Stock found that the Power Buzzer had been left halfway, without orders. Eventually the Power Buzzer was set to work, but the Amplifier was unable to receive signals owing to the noise.

(3) The Amplifier moved forward to the gun pits at N8c8.3. and received signals from the Power Buzzer at N15d5.3. (about 1700 yards).

(4) When the 41st Infantry Brigade moved to the Command Post at N15d5.3. the Amplifier was taken with it, but received no signals from the Buzzer which had gone forward with the Battalion.

Lieut Stock went in search of the Battalion, but was unable to find the Buzzer.

(5) No message was sent by Power Buzzer, as Telephonic communication was maintained practically without interruption, except in the case described in para 4.

(6) The following difficulties were encountered in establishing communication ;-

    (a) Transportation. Heavy loads over rough ground.

    (b) Accumulators required charging. Owing to shortage we had to send back to Achicourt for fresh accumulators. This took 5 hours. Meantime the Amplifier was out of action.

    (c) Necessity of a dugout for the Amplifier, to keep it dry, and to have silence.

    (d) Inexperienced Operators both of Power Buzzer and Amplifier.

    (e) Power Buzzer Operators being left without instructions.

From the above it may be concluded that this means of communication is not suited for work beyond the Trench System, but that within the limits of the Trenches it may prove invaluable, provided the personnel is thoroughly trained. To ensure success, an Officer must accompany each Power Buzzer.

Aeroplane Contact. Messages to Aeroplanes do not appear to have been sent, as other communication was generally available, and Battalions had received instructions that they were only to signal to Aeroplanes in an emergency.

Ground Sheets and Strips were in most cases put out.

Major R.E.
Commanding 14th Signal Co.R.E.

SECRET
===========

14th Division
S.G. 2584.

14th DIVISION SIGNAL COMMUNICATIONS FOR THE OFFENSIVE.

1. **Diagrams and Map.**

    (i). The accompanying diagrams Nos. 1 and 2 show the various means of communication which will be established at Zero and after the capture of the Blue Line.

    (ii). The Map No. 3 shows the existing system in advance of the Advanced Divisional Exchange in CHRISTCHURCH Cave and the proposed extensions to TELEGRAPH HILL.

2. **Buried Cable Routes.**

    All cable routes East of DAINVILLE and as far as Advanced Brigade Command Posts are buried at least 6 ft. deep or are laid in tunnels or sewers.

3. **Communication by telephone and telegraph.**

    A. Artillery.

    The Group Exchange will be in CHRISTCHURCH Cave, providing telephonic and telegraphic communication from C.R.A. to Groups.
    There is no O.P. Exchange, each battery having a direct line to its O.P. For observation after the capture of the objectives each Group will have an O.P. line put through as far as LOWEN SCHANZE, or further according to progress made, before Z day, and these lines will be extended by ground lines as soon as possible.

    B. Infantry.

    Each of the Infantry Brigades is in direct communication with the Division and each has an alternative route through the Advanced Exchange in CHRISTCHURCH Cave.
    Before Zero the battalions of the assaulting Infantry Brigades will be connected through to their respective Advanced Brigade Command Posts.
    During the advance to the Blue Line Advanced Signal Stations will be established at approximately M 6 d 4.3 for the left brigade, and M 12 d 8.5 for the right brigade. Wires will be run out to these stations from each Advanced Brigade Command Post. An exchange will be established at each of these advanced stations and battalions should run out lines to them as soon as the situation permits.

4. **Liaison between Infantry and Artillery.**

    The Artillery Liaison Officer with each Infantry Brigade will be connected to the Group Exchange. The two F.O.Os. will be in direct telephonic communication with their respective Liaison Officers.

5. **Runners.**

    As soon as the situation permits, runner posts will be established as follows :-

    Left Bde.   No.1. Advanced Brigade Command Post.
                No.2. Junction of TELEGRAPH LANE and
                      CORDITE TRENCH (M 6 a 3.5).
                No.3. Advanced Signal Station (M 6 d 4.3).

    Right Bde. No.1. Advanced Brigade Command Post.
                No.2. M 11 b 9.3.
                No.3. M 12 d 1.4.
                No.4. Advanced Signal Station (M 12 d 8.5).

    All Runner Posts will be marked by notice boards, and routes marked by sign posts.

- 2 -

6. **Visual Signalling.**
The central receiving station is at G 35 a 1.3 (call V S) and two transmitting stations are at M 5 a 70.05 (call K R) and M 5 b 6.9 (call Z D B). Two receiving stations for forward work are being established at M 5 d 7.3 (call Z D C) and M 5 b 6.9 (call Z D B). The receiving station Z D C and transmitting station K R will be connected by telephone. When the first objective has been carried, each Brigade will establish an advanced signal station, the left brigade at M 6 d 4.3 (call B P) and the right brigade at M 12 d 8.5 (call Z Z).

For the advance from the Blue to the Brown Line a receiving station (call T S) will be established on TELEGRAPH HILL about N 7 c 1.9. Communication from T S to Z Z will be by runner till other arrangements can be made.

Battalions will send their messages to these stations by runner, for transmission.

7. **Pigeons.**
The Pigeon Loft to be used by this Division is close to SIMENCOURT and is connected by telephone to the Divisional Exchange.

A forward dump of pigeons, probably not more than 4 pairs, will be established at G 35 a 0.7. It is hoped to be able to supply the Right Brigade with 6 pairs of birds and the Left Brigade with 4 pairs.

Messages arriving at the Loft will be telephoned to the Divisional Signal Office and sent by telegraph to addressee.

8. **Power Buzzer.**
(i). An Amplifier is to be installed at LOWEN SCHANZE. Each Brigade will be allotted a Power Buzzer which should be sent forward with a selected Battalion Commander. The calls for these Power Buzzers will be - Right Brigade C Q, and Left Brigade C S. Four signallers who have undergone a Wireless course should be appointed to operate and carry the Buzzer.

(ii). For the advance from the Blue to the Brown Line, a second Amplifier will be sent forward as far as possible. The advancing battalion will take one Power Buzzer (call C R) forward to work back to the Amplifier. Base lines must in all cases be parallel to a North and South line

9. **Wireless.**
A Trench Wireless Set, sending and receiving, will be placed at the disposal of each Brigade Commander. These sets will work back to the Corps directing station near ACHICOURT. An officer and four men who have undergone a Wireless Course, must be detailed to carry each set and encode and decode messages.

The calls for these sets are - Right Brigade Y M, Left Brigade Y M M and for Corps directing station YU.

10. **Aeroplane Contact.**
Signalling from the front line will be by Flares in accordance with orders to be issued later.

Battalions and Brigades will carry with them the following equipment :-
French Lamp or Signalling Panel.
Ground Signalling Sheet.
Signalling Strips.
Flares as ordered.

Three signallers must be detailed to carry and operate this equipment, and must keep in close touch with the Battalion Commander so that he may avail himself of the

/opportunity

opportunity when a contact aeroplane is overhead.

The distinguishing mark of the contact aeroplane is - Black band beneath the lower starboard plane, with a streamer behind.

The sending of messages to aeroplanes is only to be used in case of emergency, when other means are not available.

Messages are to be confined to the code laid down on page 71 of S.S.135.

11. **Supply of Equipment.**

(i). An advanced Signal dump under an officer detailed by 14th Div. Signal Coy. will be made at G 35 a 0.7. Pigeons, cable, and other stores will be available here.

Artillery Brigades, Infantry Brigades and Battalions can draw on this dump on a written indent signed by the Signalling Officer concerned.

(ii). Smaller dumps of cable will be made at the Advanced Brigade Command Posts.

Lieut Colonel
General Staff
14th (Light) Division

April 2nd, 1917.

Copies to -

14th Div. Artillery.
41st Infantry Brigade
42nd Infantry Brigade
43rd Infantry Brigade
C. R. E.
14th Div. Signal Coy.
11th King's Liverpool Regt.
Q Branch.
A.D.M.S.
D.A.D.O.S.
A.P.M.
Div. Gas Officer.
VII Corps.
VII Corps H.A.
56th Division
3rd Division.

SECRET

14th Division
S.G.2674.

14th Division Signal Communications for the Offensive, forwarded under No. S.G.2584 of April 2nd, 1917, are amended as follows :-

Delete para.7 and substitute -

The pigeon loft to be used by this Division is in ARRAS, and connected by telephone to CHRISTCHURCH CAVE exchange.
Messages arriving at the loft will be telephoned direct to the addressee.

Delete para.8 (ii), and substitute -

For the advance from the Blue to the Brown Line at plus 7 hours the Amplifier at LOWEN SCHANZE will be moved forward as far as possible. 42nd Inf. Bde. must be informed when this move takes place. The advancing battalion of the 43rd Inf. Bde. will take forward one power buzzer (call C R) to work back to the Amplifier. Runners must be detailed to go with the Amplifier to carry messages back to the Advanced Signal Station.

(iii). Base lines must in all cases be parallel to a North and South line.

Delete the calls in para. 9 and substitute -

        Calls for the Wireless Sets will be -

            Right Bde. ..   Y M
            Left Bde. ..   Y M K
            Corps Directing
               Station ..   Y Ü

E. R. Meade-Walde
Major
for
Lieut Colonel
General Staff
14th (Light) Division

April 7th, 1917.

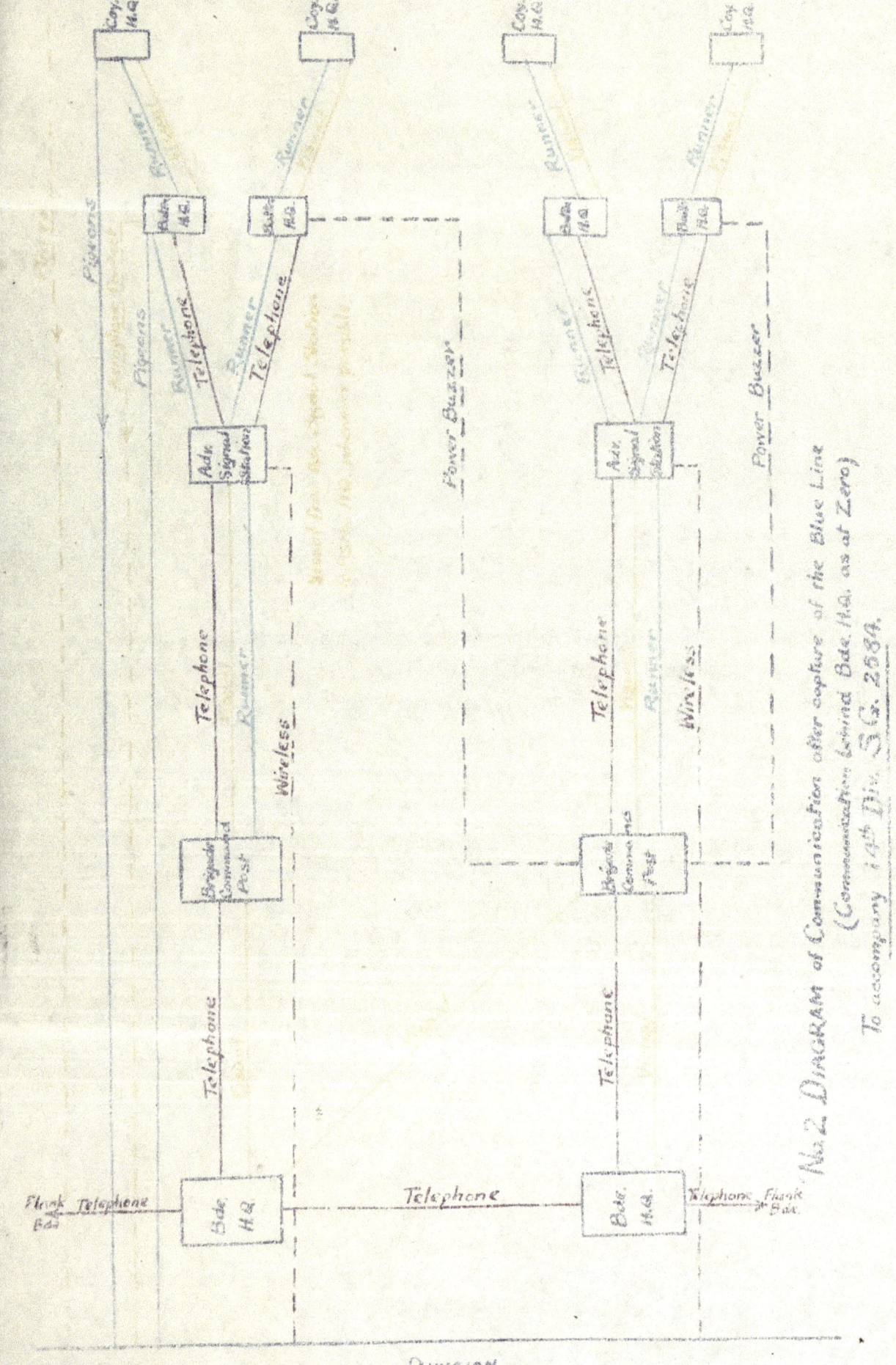

Confidential.

War Diary
of the
14th Signal Co. R.E.
From 1st to 31st May 1917.

(Volume 24.)

Army Form C. 2118.

WAR DIARY
or
INTELLIGENCE SUMMARY.

(Erase heading not required.)

MAY 1917.

14th SIGNAL COMPANY

Place	Date	Hour	Summary of Events and Information	Remarks and references to Appendices
	1st and 2nd		The Signal Company was engaged in making final preparations for the offensive to take place on May 3rd. See "Scheme of Communications" attached. Also the diagram of lines for infantry and artillery. Lines from Divn. to Brigades were of poles cables (two alternative routes) from Brigade to Advanced Brigade Headquarters lines were laid along the ground, each Brigade having as announced him, with a pair of twisted D5's common to both, as well as a lateral between Brigades. When the three forward pairs were available for communication to either Brigade. An intermediate test point (B.K.) was established into which all lines were led and where lineman were stationed. A direct line was provided from the Artillery Liaison officer with Infantry Brigades to the CRA to the Artillery "a forward exchange (CC)" was established, with 3 pairs to the Divn. and pairs to each Brigade. A quick line was found necessary between G officer and the CRA to ensure instantaneous communication of information. The attack was launched, and progressed well at first, but was soon driven back to where it began. The enemy put up a barrage over the COTEUL Valley which cut all lines continuously. Linemen were working continuously on these lines, and except for a very short period one pair at least was always kept through. During the short period mentioned when all lines were down, messages were sent by runner from Advanced Bde HdQrs to Divison. An 'SOS' message came through by this means during this period.	
	3.			

WAR DIARY
or
INTELLIGENCE SUMMARY.

(Erase heading not required.)

Army Form C. 2118.

Place	Date	Hour	Summary of Events and Information	Remarks and references to Appendices
	4.		The forward visual station was shelled intermittently, but communication was maintained continuously (distance 5,500 yards). The "Bds" were unable to establish their forward Signal Station as arranged. The 42nd pushed forward the men to do so, but the whole station was blown up. The 43rd were unable to maintain communication to their forward station. Brigades finally established a R forward station as far advanced as possible, and concentrated on maintaining one line to this station. Battalions in some cases laid out lines, but these were cut to ribbons. Visual signalling was impossible on the forward slope owing to the heavy shelling and machine gun fire. Runners were used on the heavy zone, but with great difficulty. The heavy shelling of the 3rd proved that a single line to advanced Brigade Headquarters could not be maintained. So work was started on making a laddered line by putting rungs across two of the existing lines, rungs being about 30 yards apart. This line eventually proved satisfactory, though requiring a lot of maintenance.	
	5.		The 43rd Brigade relieved the 41st & 42nd Brigade in the line. The 3rd Bde	

Army Form C. 2118.

WAR DIARY
or
INTELLIGENCE SUMMARY.
(Erase heading not required.)

Instructions regarding War Diaries and Intelligence Summaries are contained in F.S. Regs., Part II. and the Staff Manual respectively. Title pages will be prepared in manuscript.

Place	Date	Hour	Summary of Events and Information	Remarks and references to Appendices
	6-10		Headquarters remained at N21a8.6. So they had only one pair to ZDB, lines were hastily run out from ZDB & ZDC on the ground, to connect ZDC to 4th Battalions. Wire Companies spent next day. Exerted chiefly to improving the forward lines, and laying out lines to companies.	
	11		43rd Brigade took over extra frontage of 500 yards from the 18th Division on our right. One Battalion Headquarters was established at N30b6.3. This was connected by running a pair of D5 cables to BK. An exchange was put in at BK in order to better utilise the various forward lines, instead of continually cross connecting them.	
	14/15		A&1 Brigade relieved 43rd Bde. No change in arrangement of communication.	
	18.		Division moved to new Headquarters to N23a6.5. The Officers Mess and N7a4.0 closed down. From the new H.Q. the Corps built a 4 pair communications to connect to the system of lines which had been used by the 8th Division, who had moved. Here lines were led into the Brigade and Artillery exchange offices. Communication to Corps and flanking divisions was obtained o/c permanent route passing Headquarters.	
	19		The Signal Company built a pole cable (2 pair twisted D5) running north of NEUVILLE VITASSE to Brigade Headquarters. Below of forward communication this consisted of a) 4 pair comm; 2 pair to Bde Headquarters, 2 pair & artillery exchange,	

WAR DIARY
or
INTELLIGENCE SUMMARY.

(Erase heading not required.)

Army Form C. 2118.

Place	Date	Hour	Summary of Events and Information	Remarks and references to Appendices
	20-24		and B) 2 pair poled cable, one to Bde Hd Qrs and one to Artillery exchange. Picking up the old cable lines abandoned on leaving the old Sector.	
	24		Building a room to BEAURAINS to mount the Brigade there.	
	27.		42nd Brigade relieved 46th Bde on the line. No change of system of communications. Mobile Cyclo-tofft No.21, near NEUVILLE VITASSE, brought into use by the Division and connected to the Brigade exchange there.	
	/19		A new exchange was established at AGNY, connected to the Simmone exchange. The exchange was reconnected to the Divl Exam, DAC, etc. The exchange room was also used as a Bgde Signal Office to deal with messages and dispatches for all units in AGNY.	

A Everard
Major RE
OC 14th Signal
OC 14th Signal Co.

SECRET   14th Division
                                    S.G.2810.

SCHEME FOR COMMUNICATIONS DURING FORTHCOMING OPERATIONS

Telephone 1. All Brigades will be connected by telephone to the Division. The Division and Brigades in the front line will be connected to Divisions and Brigades on their flanks.
  Advanced Signal Stations will be established by 41st Inf. Bde. at O 26 b 2.8 (call GC), by 42nd Inf. Bde. at O 20 c 5.5 (call ST). The above stations will be connected to their respective Advanced Bde. H.Q. by telephone. Advanced Battalion Command Posts when formed should be connected to these stations.

Mounted Orderlies and Runners. 2. Mounted orderlies will be established at Advanced Div. H.Q. at 42nd Bde. H.Q. at N 15 d 5.2 and at H.Q. Reserve Battn. Right Brigade at N 24 c 0.5, as soon as the Red Line is captured the latter post will be moved to Adv. Bde. H.Q., O 19 a 2.2 (N.B. Adv. H.Q. of both 41st and 42nd Inf. Bdes. are together at O 19 a 2.2). Runners will be kept at N 24 c 0.5 to carry messages to Adv. Bde. H.Q. when required.

Visual 3. Visual communication by Lamp and Helio will be maintained between Adv. Div. H.Q. and Adv. Bde. H.Q., and between 41st Bde. H.Q. at N 22 d 5.7 and Reserve Battn. H.Q. at N 24 c 0.5. 41st Inf. Bde. will establish a receiving station at O 26 b 2.8 (call GC) and 42nd Inf. Bde. at O 20 c 5.5 (call ST).

Amplifier and Power Buzzer. 4. The Amplifier will remain at Adv. Bde. H.Q. O 19 a 2.2. Power Buzzers will be at ST and GC. The Amplifier and Power Buzzers will not move unless an advance from the Red Line is ordered.

Wireless 5. Wireless communication will be maintained between a Trench Set at N 15 d 3.3 and another at Adv. Bde. H.Q. at O 19 a 2.2. This will not move unless an advance from the Red Line is ordered.

Pigeons 6. 41st and 42nd Inf. Bdes. will each be supplied with six pairs of pigeons. A reserve of pigeons will be at 41st Bde. H.Q. at N 22 d 5.7. Should 43rd Inf. Bde. be ordered forward they will collect all available pigeons from this dump.

Contact Aeroplanes 7. Arrangements as for the previous offensive. The markings on the planes are unchanged.

Dump 8. A dump of pigeons, cable and other signal stores will be at N 22 d 5.7.

Artillery 9. An Advanced Artillery Exchange connected to 14th Div. Artillery has been formed at N 22 c 7.4 to which all Groups are connected. Artillery Liaison Officers at Adv. Bde. H.Qs. are connected by telephone to Adv. R.A. Exchange, and by visual to Adv. Div. H.Q.

                                 Lieut Colonel
                                 General Staff
                               14th (Light) Division

May 2nd, 1917.

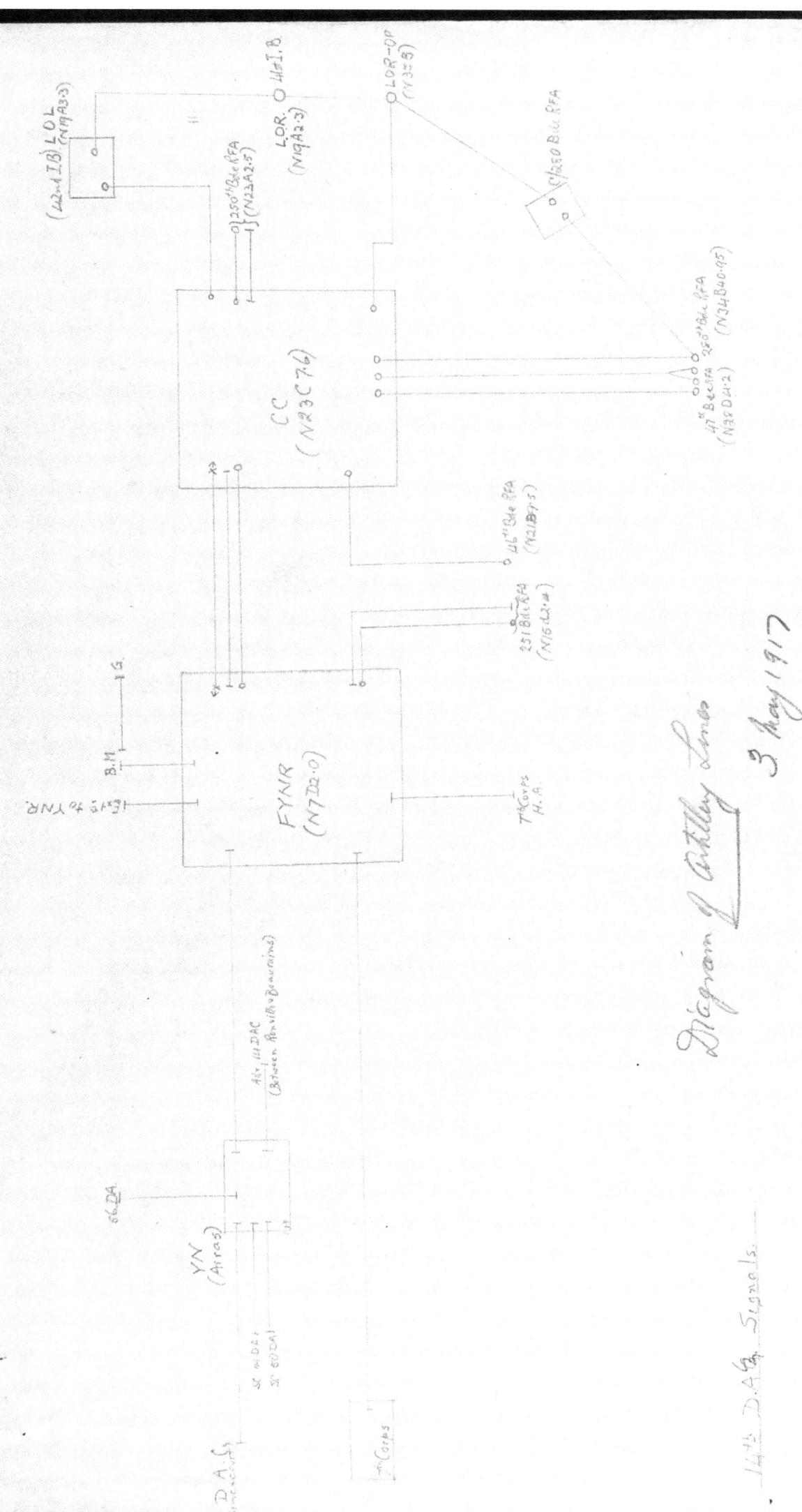

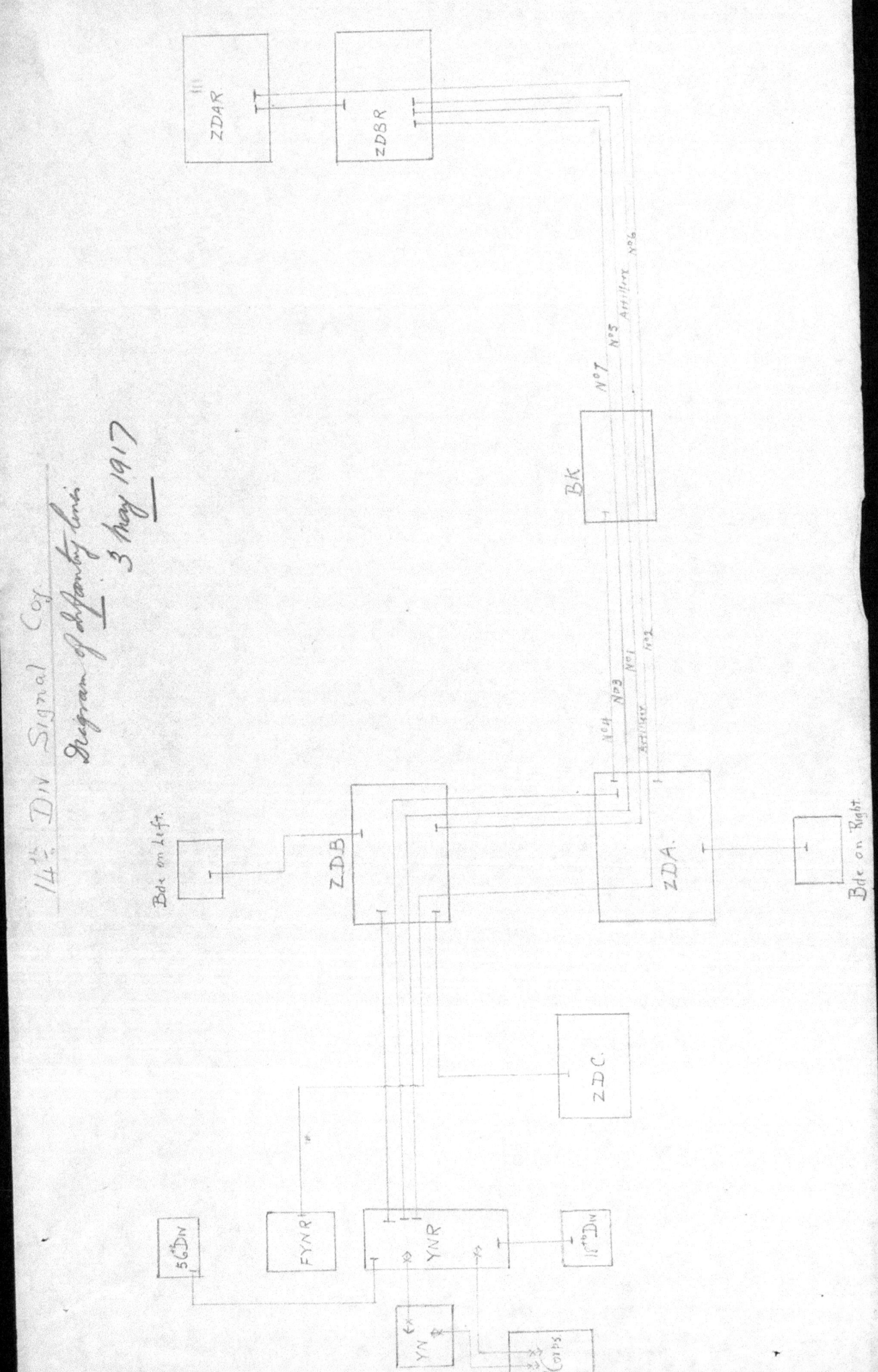

Vol 21

Confidential.

War Diary
of the
14th Signal Company R.E.
From 1st to 30th June 1917.
(Volume — 25.)

WAR DIARY or INTELLIGENCE SUMMARY

Army Form C. 2118.

Place	Date	Hour	Summary of Events and Information	Remarks and references to Appendices
	JUNE 3		A class of instructional Battalion and R.F.A. Signallers assembled at the 14th Divisional Depot at BREVILLERS. The class numbered 86. The instructors consisted of one Officer from the Signal Company and 8 O.R's. A programme of work was prepared to cover 6 weeks.	
	4.		42nd Brigade relieved 43rd Brigade in the line. Arrangements for communication remained the same. During the first week of the month considerable work was done in improving the aerial route from Division to Brigade.	
			The Pigeon loft was connected direct to the Brigade on the line, and messages were received at Brigade from the trenches by this means in about 10 minutes.	
	9		Brigade began to move to back feed area. Communication was maintained during the move by M.C. despatch rider.	
	10.		Divisional Headquarters moved to Chateau at MARIEUX. Communication obtained with 4th Corps by telephone and telegraph. The rest of the line held by the 14th Div was handed over as follows:- Left Battn to 61st Div, who ran direct lines from their Brigade Signal Office. Right Battalion Sector remained held by 43rd Brigade, who passed under command of 18th Div. Communication was established by linking 43rd Bde to the existing system of 18th Div. The Artillery passed to command of 18th Div, who ran lines to the Group from their Arty Exchange.	
	11		42nd Brigade arrived at BEAUQUESNE. Communication established by telephone	

WAR DIARY or INTELLIGENCE SUMMARY

Army Form C. 2118.

Place	Date	Hour	Summary of Events and Information	Remarks and references to Appendices
	13.		41st Brigade arrived at LOUVENCOURT	
	15.		43rd Brigade arrived at AUTHIE, having been relieved in the line by units of 18th Divn and marched to rest area.	
	15 to 30		Communication by Telephone was established with both Brigades. Classes of instruction were started at Divisional Headquarters for personnel of the Signal Company, with the object of improving their technical knowledge and to find with examination for remustering and retrating. Classes were as follows:- 1) Operating. 2) Linemen and work 3) Knowledge of instruments and Office working. 4) Cable cart work. These classes were very necessary in view of the very limited training received by reinforcements now arriving from the Signal Depot.	
	28.		The Artillery of the Division commenced a march to a northern area. The following were detailed to accompany the CRA:- The Office to Artillery communication, the RA Headquarters detachment of the Signal Company, and one cable detachment. Instrument and stores proportionate to their assignment were carried in their G.S. wagon.	

Trumpf Major RE
OC 14th Signal Co.

Confidential.

War Diary
of the
14th Signal Co. R.E.
From July 1-31. 1917.
Volume 26.

WAR DIARY
or
INTELLIGENCE SUMMARY

Army Form C. 2118.

July 1917.

Date	Hour	Summary of Events and Information	Remarks and references to Appendices
1st to 10th		Training continued as laid down in August Diary. On 8th the class of signallers at Lynde Befft was concluded. From 2nd to 8th a class was held for all Battalion Signalling Officers.	
11th		Artillery Headquarters moved by road to 9th Corps area. R.A. H.Q. Detachment, and one detachment of "No 1 Section moved with it. The Company moved from MARIEUX to ST JANS CAPPEL. The move commenced by a march to DOULLENS, where entrainment took place, leaving about 2 h.e.c. The train arrived at BAILLEUL at about 5 am, detrainment lasted about two hours, the Company then marched to ST JANS CAPPEL. The Signal Office closed at MARIEUX at 9 am, the party remaining coming to new Hd Qrs by lorry. An advance party opened office at new Hd Qrs when at MONT NOIR already existed, and lines to Brigades were put through on existing permanent lines as follows: 41st Bde to MONT KOKEREELE R16 b.6.5, 42nd Bde to Sheet 28 S7 B.6.4, 43rd Bde to M20 D.5.5.	
13th to 31st		14th Q.rs did not move. Training particularly in auxiliary means of communication was carried out. Wireless instruction included general training of operators of the Company, and of Battalion Signallers in use of Power Buzzer. Also a demonstration of the U.T, Fullerphone, Power Buzzer &c what was attended by most officers of Battalions and by Battalion Signallers.	

Lundy Major R.E.
OC 14th Signal Co.

Confidential.

War Diary
of the
14th Signal Co. R.E.

August 1st – 31st 1917.

Volume 27.

WAR DIARY or INTELLIGENCE SUMMARY.

AUGUST 1917

(Erase heading not required.)

Place	Date	Hour	Summary of Events and Information	Remarks and references to Appendices
	1-6		No change in Headquarters or system of communication. Classification of all Battalion Signallers begun.	
	6		2nd Headquarters less Artillery move to CAESTRE. 41st Brigade to HONDEGHEM, 42nd Brigade to BORRE, 43rd Brigade to CAESTRE. Class Pistol examination of Battalion Signallers continued.	
	15		2nd Headquarters moved to RENINGHELST, and Brigades to camps nearby. Telephone communication established with the 3 Brigades.	
	18		The Division relieved 50th Division in the line (frontage WESTHOEK to INVERNESS COPSE, Divion Headquarters to Sheet 28, H27b6.8. 41st Brigade Headquarters at DORMY HOUSE I23c6.4, and 42nd Bde. at HALFWAY HOUSE. Telephone communication to both Brigades by alternative routes or buried cables. R.A. Headquarters joined Division Headquarters, and communication opened with the 5 groups of Artillery in the line.	
	19th 20 21 22		Preparing communications for offensive operations. Working party at BEDFORD HOUSE.	
	22		41st Brigade relieved in the line by 43rd Brigade. Attack began at 7a.m. on Inverness Copse and Glencorse Wood. The scheme of communications for the attack, and note on these communications are attached.	
	25		43rd Brigade relieved in the line by the 41st Brigade.	
	26		41st Brigade took over frontage of 42nd Brigade. Forward communication headquarters to route on left about has been shelled. 42nd Brigade moved back to THIEUSHOOK. 14th Division relieved by 23rd Division, who took over existing system of communication.	

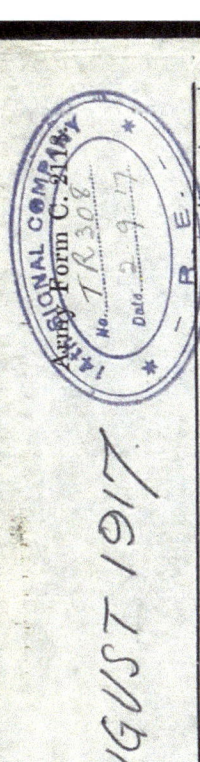

WAR DIARY
or
INTELLIGENCE SUMMARY.
(Erase heading not required.)

Army Form C. 2118/y
No. TR 308
Date 2-7-17
SIGNAL COMPANY
R.E.

Instructions regarding War Diaries and Intelligence Summaries are contained in F.S. Regs., Part II. and the Staff Manual respectively. Title pages will be prepared in manuscript.

Place	Date	Hour	Summary of Events and Information	Remarks and references to Appendices
	29	4 pm	41st Brigade remained in the line; CRA remained in command of Artillery, the O/C Div Artillery Signals, Headquarters detachment and one cable detachment being left with 23rd Division. Divisional Headquarters moved back to REININGHELST. 43rd Brigade Headquarters near Reninghelst and in telephone communication with Division. Divisional Headquarters moved to BERTHEN, and communication obtained with II Anzac Corps. 43rd Brigade moved to ROCKLOSHILLE, Sheet 27, x 1. Arrangements	
	30.		41st Brigade moved to METEREN, having been relieved in the line by a Brigade of the 23rd Division. Telephone communication now established with all three Brigades.	

Kennedy Major RE
O.C. 14th Sig Co

F,

SIGNAL COMMUNICATIONS FOR THE OFFENSIVE.

To accompany 14th Division Operation Order No. 135.

Reference Sheet ZILLEBEKE
1/10,000.

The following arrangements will be in force at ZERO :-

(1). Division to Brigades.

(a). Telephone.

Telephonic communication is arranged to 42nd and 43rd Brigades by alternative routes with lateral communication between the two Brigades and to Brigades on both flanks.

(b). Visual.

Visual communication is arranged from a station at I 17 c 5.1 to BEDFORD HOUSE. The station at I 17 c 5.1 is connected to both Brigades by telephone and runner. BEDFORD HOUSE is connected by direct telephone to Division.

(c). Wireless.

A wireless station is erected at each Brigade H.Q. and these are in communication with the Corps Directing Station at H 22 c 5.8, which is connected to Division by telephone.

(d). Despatch Rider Service.

Motor Cyclist D.Rs. run from the Division to a D.R. station at I 9 d 5.4, from which place the despatches are relayed on to Brigades by runner. The D.R. post is connected by telephone to Division and 42nd Brigade H.Q.
Motor Cyclist D.Rs. are stationed at the D.R. Post for special despatches from Brigades to Division. Commencing at ZERO regular D.R. posts will cease and only specials will be run.
All important despatches will be sent in duplicate.

(e). Pigeons.

Two pairs of pigeons will be kept at each Brigade H.Q.

(2). Brigades to Battalions.

(a). 42nd Brigade.

A Brigade forward station is at I 13 a 8.2 adjacent to both Battalion H.Q. and connected to Brigade H.Q. by telephone, visual, wireless and runner.
An Amplifier at this station will receive messages from 2 Power Buzzers, one with each Battalion to be installed near the front line.

(b). 43rd Brigade.

A Brigade forward station is at J 19 a 8.9 connected to Brigade H.Q. by telephone, visual, wireless and runner.
An Amplifier is installed at this station for receiving messages from 2 Power Buzzers to be taken forward, one by each Battalion in line.

/2.

- 2 -

(3). <u>Artillery.</u>

   Telephonic communication exists to all Artillery Groups, and these are connected laterally.
   In the event of a Group being out of communication with Artillery H.Q., messages may be sent from Infantry Brigade H.Q. or from the visual station at I 17 c 5.1.

(4). <u>Pigeons.</u>

   There is a plentiful supply of these.
   2 pairs to be kept at Brigade H.Q., 2 pairs with each Battalion in line, and 2 pairs with Companies of each Battalion.
   The pigeon loft is connected to Divisional H.Q. by telephone.

(5). <u>Signal Stations.</u>

   The following are the Signal Stations in the area :-

42nd Brigade H.Q.	HALFWAY HOUSE.
43rd Brigade H.Q.	DORMY HOUSE.
D.R. Post	I 9 d 5.4.
BEDFORD HOUSE	I 26 a 9.4.
42nd Brigade Forward Station	I 13 a 8.2.
43rd Brigade Intermediate Station	I 24 b 2.7.
43rd Brigade Forward Station	J 19 a 8.9.

(6). <u>Miscellaneous.</u>

   The Aeroplane Dropping Ground is at Divisional H.Q.
   A Cable Dump exists at I 9 d 5.4 (D.R. Post.)
   When Battalions in the line are relieved, they will hand over to incoming Battalions all pigeons, pigeon equipment and Power Buzzers.
   After ZERO Power Buzzer messages may be sent in clear, but wireless messages must be sent in special wireless cipher.
   Enciphering and deciphering is done by the wireless personnel.

NOTES ON SIGNAL COMMUNICATIONS DURING OPERATIONS.
22 - 25 August 1917.

The system of communications outlined in schedule F accompanying 14th Divisional Operation Order No 135 was established at ZERO.

(1) **Telephonic Communication.**

    (a) <u>Division to Brigades.</u>
The lines from Division to Brigades were cut on several occasions, but as there were alternative routes to each, uninterrupted communication was maintained. Laterals were cut frequently, and it was not always possible to repair these at once, as all available personnel was engaged in maintaining forward lines.

    (b) <u>Brigades to Battalions.</u>
In the case of both Brigades the enemy barrage was put down between Brigade and Battalion H.Q. and it was not possible to maintain any line through this barrage. From Brigade H.Q. up to the line of the barrage one line was maintained throughout by each Brigade, and messages sent by telephone on these lines, and then relayed on by runner.

(2) **Despatch Rider Service.**

The system of sending despatches by Motor Cyclist D.R. to the Runner Post, and then on by runner, worked satisfactorily, and caused little delay.

(3) **Visual.**

    (a) <u>Bedford House to Brigade H.Q.</u>
Visual communication was maintained throughout, but was not required, as telephonic communication did not break down.

    (b) <u>Left Brigade.</u>
Visual communication was established from Brigade H.Q. to Battalion H.Q. and to one forward Company H.Q. but did not work continuously, due to smoke of barrage, and to heavy shelling of Battalion Station.
The Company Station was working satisfactorily, but was removed by order of the Company Commander.

    (c) <u>Right Brigade.</u>
Visual to both Battalion H.Q. was successfully maintained, except for short intervals, when shelling of the stations threw lamps out of alignment, or destroyed them.

(4) **Pigeons.**

Pigeons provided the quickest method of getting messages back from the front line.
About 12 messages were received on the 22nd, and 18 on the 24th, many of which reached Divisional H.Q. in 25 minutes, or less.
One Sketch Map was sent by pigeon, and this means of transmitting information might well be developed.
The Pigeons flew well, even in bad weather.

(5) <u>Wireless.</u>

The stations at Brigade H.Q. successfully maintained communication with the Corps Directing Station, but forward stations were not possible to maintain.

(6) <u>Amplifier and Power Buzzer.</u>

    (a) <u>Left Brigade.</u>
        The Amplifier was at Battalion H.Q. and 2 Power Buzzers were set up in the front line.
        Messages were received from these Power Buzzers, but as the Amplifier base lines were continually cut by shells communication was not reliable.

    (b) <u>Right Brigade.</u>
        The 2 Amplifier stations established communication with each other, but it was not possible to maintain the base line of the forward station.
        2 Power Buzzers went forward to the fron line, but these appear to have been lost in the fighting.

(7) <u>Runners.</u>

Runners were very hard worked throughout the fighting, but took a long time to get back.
Forward of Battalions they were the only means of getting forward information, and took about 2 hours from Battalion H.Q. to front line.
From Battalion H.Q. to Brigade H.Q. the time averaged about $\frac{3}{4}$ hour.

<u>Lessons to be Learned.</u>

    (a) It is useless to endeavour to maintain a ground line through the barrage. Even a ladder line is cut to pieces. The line should be terminated ~~on a line~~ clear of the barrage, and messages relayed on by runner.

    (b) <u>Cover for Visual Stations.</u>
        This is necessary to give confidence to the Signallers and to prevent lamps being thrown out of alignment..

    (c) Amplifier base line should be buried when possible.

    (d) Plenty of pigeons are required and plenty of men trained in their use.
        Pigeon maps might with advantage be printed and distributed with the pigeons.
        At ZERO a pigeon dump should be formed as far forward as possible.

    (e) Runner Posts and Signal Stations should be marked by <u>luminous</u> signs.
        Much time is wasted by runners at night, in finding the Runner Posts.

August 30th 1917.

Major R.E.
Cmdg 14th Divl Signal CoR.E

Vol 24

Confidential.

War Diary
of the
14th Signal Co R E
September 1-30. 1917.

Volume 28.

Army Form C. 2118.

WAR DIARY
INTELLIGENCE SUMMARY.
(Erase heading not required.)

Instructions regarding War Diaries and Intelligence Summaries are contained in F.S. Regs., Part II. and the Staff Manual respectively. Title pages will be prepared in manuscript.

Place	Date	Hour	Summary of Events and Information	Remarks and references to Appendices
Field	1917 1st Sept		Division HQ at BERTHEN Communication with 41st Inf Bde at METEREN ⎫ By telephone with sounder " " 42nd " at THIEUSHOEK ⎬ superimposed through " " 43rd " at LEROUKLOSHILLE. ⎭ permanent lines in II ANZAC Corps area	
	2nd		42nd Inf Bde relieved 90th Inf Bde in the line with HQ at T6c6.6 under 30th Divn. Company moved to RAVELSBERG 28 S 17 b 2.0 and opened Office for Divn HQ. Advance party for forward work under Corpl Reeves sent to L.G. dugout. Communication to 41st and 43rd Brigades through 8th Corps, which relieved II Anzac Corps.	
	3rd	10 am	The command of the 42nd Inf Bde passed to 14th Division. Lines employed by 30th Divn to 42nd Inf Bde were switched at XH on to the RCL route. The 41st Inf Bde moved to Waterloo Camp 28 S 18 D 2.2, communication direct from DivnHQ by poled cable, telephone and sounder superimposed. Party under Corpl Reeves moved to P.Q. 28 T 6 C 0.5 who reconnoitred forward lines in the buried system. Diagram of communications taken over, attached.	
	4th		43rd Inf Bde moved to La Creche area. Direct communication through permanent lines and sounder superimposed. Major Grundy on 1 months leave to United Kingdom.	

WAR DIARY
INTELLIGENCE SUMMARY.
(Erase heading not required.)

Army Form C. 2118.

Sheet 2

Instructions regarding War Diaries and Intelligence Summaries are contained in F. S. Regs., Part II. and the Staff Manual respectively. Title pages will be prepared in manuscript.

Place	Date 1917	Hour	Summary of Events and Information	Remarks and references to Appendices
Field	Sept 5th		Corpl Reeves party employed in making changes in test boxes required for new tactical lines. Work commenced by all available men on re-marking roads and horse standings and Rutments at the Horse Lines.	
	7th		1 NCO and 7 men of the 11th Kings Liverpool Regt (Pioneers) reported for training as visual signallers to be permanently attached to the Divisional Signal Co.	
	8th		14th Div Sig. took over Command of 26th and 311th A.F.A. Brigades covering our Sector.	
	8th to 15th		1 Officer & 20 other ranks of 43rd Inf Bde working on filling up shell-holes, making good and marking out the buried routes which were taken over in a very bad condition and in many cases were almost impossible to trace.	
	12th		The Brigade in line are in communication by buried route to all Battalions except the right Battalion which is connected to the buried route by 500 yds of ground line. An amplifier was installed at L.B. H.Q. of Machine Gun Coy which was in communication by telephone on the buried route with H.Q. Brigade in the line. This received from Report Power Buzzer at Right Battalion H.Q. 28 V10 a.O.8.	
	12th to 25th		Work carried out continuously on 3 sections of the buried route neither of which had more than 30% of its lines through. Shell holes were dug up and the number of pairs worka ble increased to about 70%.	

WAR DIARY
INTELLIGENCE SUMMARY
(Erase heading not required.)

Army Form C. 2118.

Sheet 3

Place	Date	Hour	Summary of Events and Information	Remarks and references to Appendices
Field	12th to 25th		operations were contemplated on the 21st in conjunction with larger operations further North. A very large amount of extra work was entailed in putting through F.A and H.A. communications.	
	14th		46th and 47th Brigades R.F.A. were moved into action under the orders of 1A.th D.A. A signal school was opened at the Divisional Depot Battalion for the training of all Signallers reinforcements coming to Infantry Battalions and also to train those Battalion Signallers who were not sufficiently trained to qualify as 1st or 2nd class Signallers.	
	17th		Trench set was established at H.Q. Brigade in line and on the 19th a further Trench set at Support Battalion. H.Q. 28 0.3 2 d.A-8, the proposed advanced Brigade H.Q.	
	18th		42nd Inf Bde moved to TROIS ROIS camp, Inter-Brigade relief were commenced carried out every 8 days entailing no change in communications from the time used	
	20th		A further trench set was established at Div. H.Q. Reinforcements have been trained in airline construction.	
	23rd		20 men were sent to VIIIth Corps Signal School for training as buried cable jointers.	
	24th		Courses were commenced at the Divisional Signal School for Battalion Signallers which last 3 days and will continue till at least 6 men per Battalion have been trained	

Army Form C. 2118.
Sheet 4.

WAR DIARY
~~INTELLIGENCE~~ SUMMARY
(Erase heading not required)

Place	Date	Hour	Summary of Events and Information	Remarks and references to Appendices
Field	1917 29 Sept		A Course for training Battalion and Battery Signallers in Powerbuzzer and Amplifier was formed at the Divisional Signal School as it was found that from recent operations there were no men at all left in Battalions trained in these subjects.	

H.W. Mead.
Capt. R.E.
.'. O.C. 14th Signal Co.
R.E

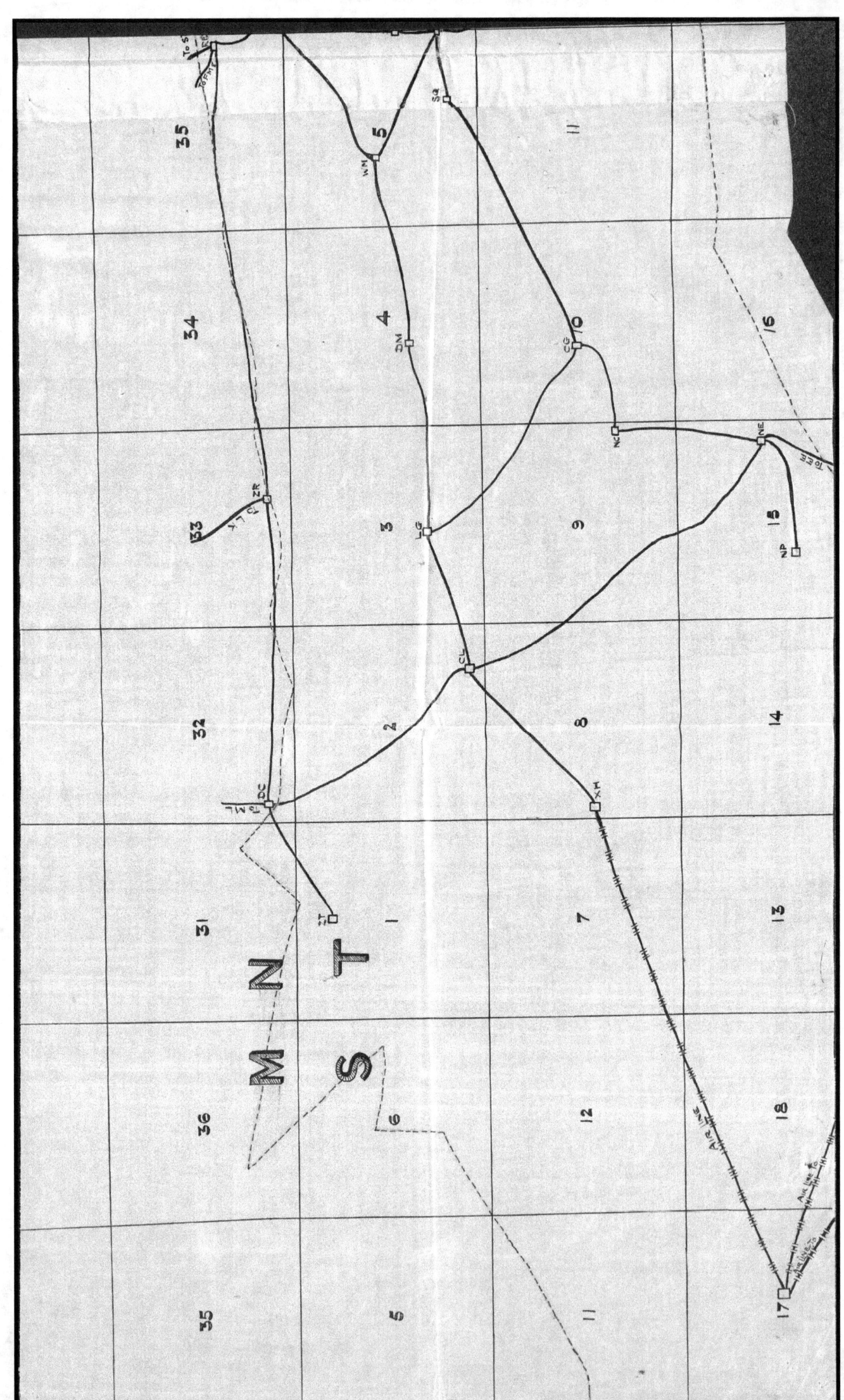

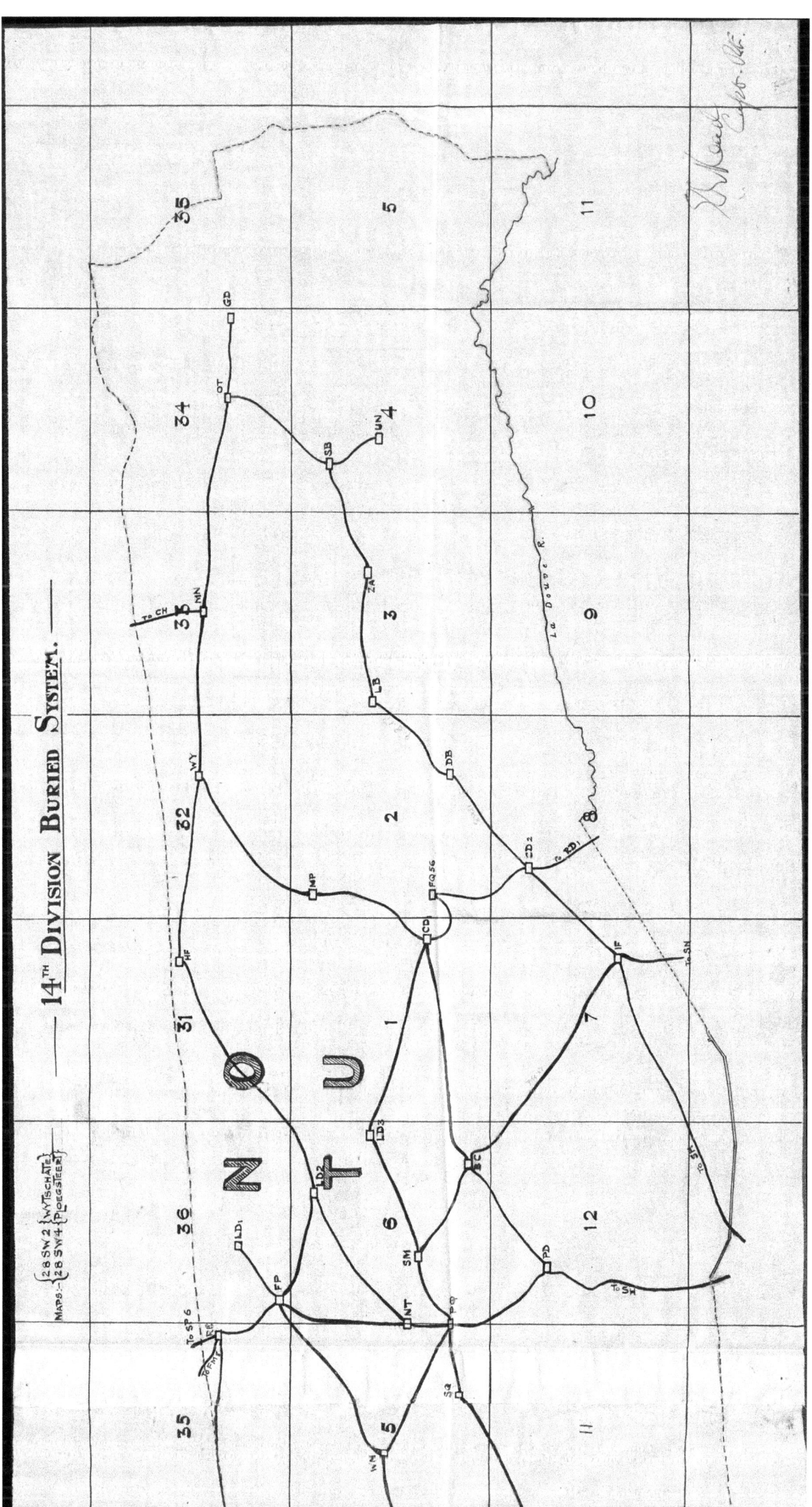

Vol 25

Confidential.

War Diary
of the
14th Signal Co R.E.

From Oct 1st — Oct 31st 1917.

Volume 29.

WAR DIARY
INTELLIGENCE SUMMARY
(Erase heading not required)

Army Form C. 2118.

Instructions regarding War Diaries and Intelligence Summaries are contained in F.S. Regs., Part II. and the Staff Manual respectively. Title pages will be prepared in manuscript.

Place	Date	Hour	Summary of Events and Information	Remarks and references to Appendices
	1st. to 8th.		Division Headquarters at RAVELSBERG, with 42nd Brigade in line, as during the last days of September.	
	9th.		Division relieved by 33rd Division. 42nd Brigade relieved by 19th Brigade. Div. Sigs. helped close at noon and opened at WESTOUTRE same time. Communication found with Xth Corps. Brigades moved up to neighbourhood of DICKEBUSH.	
	11th.	10am	14th Division relieved 5th Division at BURGOMASTER FARM. 2 Brigades in line, 41st on the right, Headquarters at 28.b.24.d.8.3, 43rd on left, Headquarters at 713.c.7.0. The system of communication taken over is outlined in attached note "Signal Comms in New Area." Maintenance of communications was a matter of some difficulty. Between Division and Brigades the buried routes were frequently cut, and continuous work was necessary in allowing connections at Test points. Forward of Brigades the Amplifier and Power Buzzer system, if that is a diagram is attached, signed continuous experience. The means of comm. was frequently interrupted by 1) lines being cut by shell fire 2) Valves being broken or amplifiers due to shock 3) Accumulators running down, due to shorting by damp. The Base lines at Hyclemens Farm, and at 715.d.4.3 were buried, the former 7 ft. deep, the latter 4½ ft. deep (no greater depth was possible owing to water). Owing to heavy shelling on Observatory Ridge, the DR post was changed to a dugout on the MENIN ROAD at I.18.d.2.6 and 2 DRs lived here. Pigeons were not much used, cupplies being limited. Visual communication was expanded, and the system established as shown in attached diagram.	

Army Form C. 2118.

WAR DIARY
or
INTELLIGENCE SUMMARY.

(Erase heading not required.)

Instructions regarding War Diaries and Intelligence Summaries are contained in F.S. Regs., Part II. and the Staff Manual respectively. Title pages will be prepared in manuscript.

Place	Date	Hour	Summary of Events and Information	Remarks and references to Appendices
	17		42nd Brigade relieved 41st Brigade in line	
	24	10am.	Command of sector handed over to 5th Division. Divion Headquarters moved to BERTHEN	
			41st Brigade to METEREN	
			42nd Brigade to THIEUSHOEK	
			43rd Brigade to 28R34c4.0.	
			Communication was obtained by telephone with 10th Corps and all Brigades.	
	30.		Experience of Amplifier working in the line had shewn that many more 8 men are required with a thorough knowledge of Amplifier working. 2 men per Battalion were therefore detailed to be attached to the Signal company for instruction.	
			Training of Battalion Signallers was begun with a view to further classification tests in the near future	

[signatures]
Lt 14th Sigs

Signal Communications in the New Area.

The following notes are forwarded for information:-

Headquarters.

Left Brigade.	J.13.c.7.0.
Forward Bde Station. (Fitzclarence Farm). Cable Head}	J.14.b.3.3.
Battalion in Line.	J.15.b.8.7.
Right Brigade.	I.24.d.8.3. (For Top).
Brigade Fwd Station.(The Tower).	J.14.d.9.4.
Left Battalion in Line.	J.15.d.5.3.
Right " " "	J.21.b.3.2

Telephone & Telegraph. At present one line exists to each Brigade by alternative routes. There is lateral communication between Brigades and to Brigades on both flanks.
Bedford House is connected by Telephone to Division, and Right Brigade.

Despatch Riders. For the present the existing scheme will be continued.
Brigade D.R's will remain at Divisional H.Q.
When a D.R. leaves for Brigades, departure will be advised by wire.
The Right Brigade will send Runners to RUDKIN HOUSE I.24.c.2.3. to meet the D.R. and take forward despatches for both Brigades.
Left Brigade will send Runners to Right Brigade to collect its despatches.
If a special is required from Brigade to Division, Brigade concerned will ask Division for a D.R. and send Runner with despatches to meet D.R. at RUDKIN HOUSE.
Till further orders D.R's will leave Division at 6am, 2pm & 6pm.

Visual. Visual will be worked from both Brigade H.Q. to a transmitting Station at YEOMANRY POST I17.d.2.3.working to BEDFORD HOUSE, whence messages are telephoned to Division.
Normally this system is to be used for routine messages only.
Attention is called to 14th Division SG669.

Pigeons. The present arrangements will be continued until further orders.
16 Pigeons per Brigade are sent up daily to RAILWAY DUG-OUTS near TRANSPORT FARM, Brigades making their own arrangements for getting them forward.
Every effort must be made to get back empty baskets.

Wireless. No Wireless will be erected at present.

Amplifier & Power Buzzer. The system of Amplifiers and Power Buzzers as shewn in the attached diagram will be taken over.
The Amplifier Stations will be manned by Operators from Division, and Power Buzzers by Signallers from Battalions.
There is an accumulator charging set at the Right Brigade H.Q.
2nd Cpl Daly will be in charge of the system in the Left Brigade, and L/Cpl Henderson in charge of the system in the Right Brigade.
These N.C.O's will live at respective Brigade H.Q.
Power Buzzers have given good results in this sector, and every effort should be made to maintain this communication.

Contact Aeroplane. Instructions will be issued later.

...gade
...munications. These consist of Runner, Power Buzzer, Visual, and
Pigeons.
In the Left Brigade there is Visual from Forward Brigade
Post to Battalion and Companies in line, and in the Right
Brigade there is Visual to Brigade Forward Station and to
Battalions.

Oct 10th 1917.

[signature]
Major R.E.
Cmdg 14th Signal Co.R.E.

14th Division. Visual Communications.

Map Ref:-
Zillebeke Sheet.
1/10,000.

——— Telephone Lines.
- - - - Visual Commⁿ.

23.10.17.

YNR.
I 28 a 9.4.
BH

I 17 d 2.2.
Y.P.

J 13 c 7.0
L. Bde.

J 13 d 8.7.
CJ

J 14 b 2.3.
FF

Bn in line.
J 15 b 87.

Res Bn.

R. Bde.
I 24 d 8.3.

J 14 d 9.3.
Spt Bn.

J 15 d 4.3.
L Bn.

J 21 63.1.
R. Bn.

Major R.E.
O.C. 14th Signal Coy.

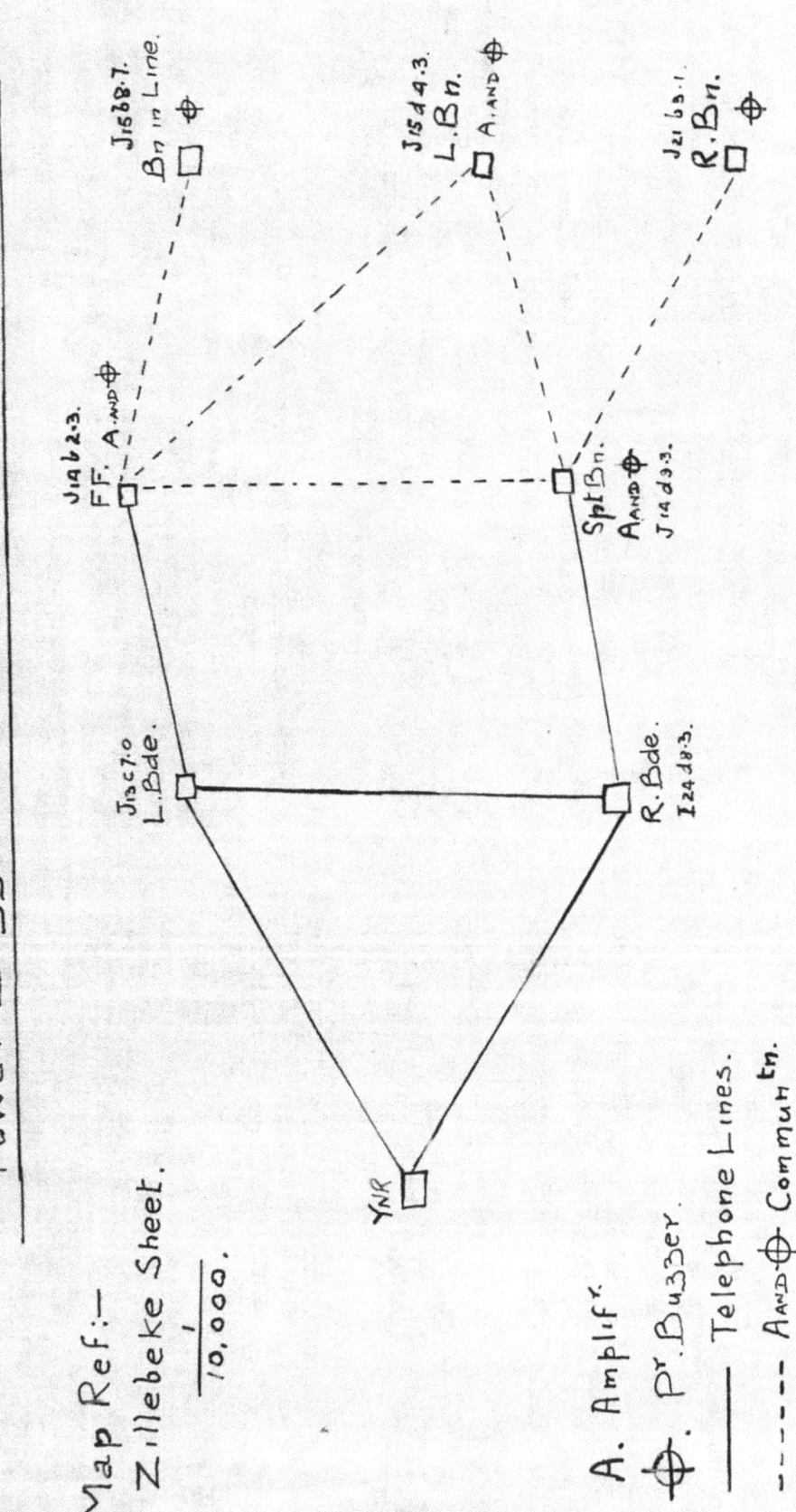

Vol 26

Confidential.

War Diary

── of the ──

14ᵀᴴ Signal Cº R.E.

From 1ˢᵗ Nov ──────── to 30ᵗʰ Nov 1917.

VOLUME. 30.

WAR DIARY or INTELLIGENCE SUMMARY

Army Form C. 2118.

November 1917

Place	Date	Hour	Summary of Events and Information	Remarks and references to Appendices
	1st to 10th		Operations as during last days of October. Training was carried out by the Company. Classes were formed for instruction in Amplifier and Power Buzzer, Wireless, Lieutenant work. N.C.O's were formed into a squad for the purpose of instruction, a drill instructor being obtained from the 6th Somerset Light Infantry for the purpose. A special squad, consisting of 12 men per Battalion, was assembled and given thorough instruction in Amplifier and Power Buzzer. The object of this was to have men trained who could help & man stations on the line, and provide responsible carrying parties. During this period the R.A. H.Q. detachment and Artillery Sub section were with their units in the line, C.R.A. being with 33rd Division. Further classification tests of Battalion Signallers were carried out. At the O.K. the Battalion of the 42nd Brigade move up for work in the Canadian Corps area. A special D.R. service to them once a day.	
	12		Company moved to TILQUES training area the company detrained at BOISLEUX and CAESTRE, detraining at WIZERNES. Divisional Headquarters opened at 1pm at WIZERNES. Communication by telephone established with ST.OMER, & working to 8th Corps, to whom Division was now temporarily attached. Communication by telephone was established with 41st Brigade at LONGUENESSE, 42nd Brigade at HALLINES, and 43rd Brigade at BOISDINGHEM. The telegraph was found to Brigades, all work being done by D.R. Lines at each Brigade	

WAR DIARY or INTELLIGENCE SUMMARY

Army Form C. 2118.

Place	Date	Hour	Summary of Events and Information	Remarks and references to Appendices
	19		There was only a telephone in the Brigade Major's Office, a DR, and sufficient runners to deliver messages to Battalions. The W/T enabled the Brigade Section to fill automan for training. Thin Hd Qrs, Nos. 1, 2, 3, 4 Sections were collected together at WIZERNES. A comprehensive programme of training was organised, to cover a period of two months, the following classes were formed:— 1) Linesman class for Drivers, to teach those drivers who showed keenness for the work. 2) Advanced Linesman class for linemen requiring further instruction in priority of special cables, testing buried cables etc. 3) Operator class to train operators from among those who showed promise, several being selected. 4) Signal Clerks class, to train operators & signallers to take charge of an office. 5) Power Buzzer & Amplifier class 6) Wireless class to train all available operators in wireless. 7, 8) Equitation and Driving Drill. In addition, Battalion signallers, numbering about 80, were assembled, and during into 6 classes. The instruction lasted a week. The object being to give a higher training to signallers, particularly in forming and use of telephone. Training was at first hampered by inoculation, too large a proportion being inoculated during the period 22nd to 26th. Towards the end of the month training had to cease, as the Division was ordered to relieve	

14th SIGNAL COMPANY

Army Form C. 2118.

WAR DIARY
or
INTELLIGENCE SUMMARY.
(Erase heading not required.)

Place	Date	Hour	Summary of Events and Information	Remarks and references to Appendices
	29		The 8th Division in the PASSCHENDAELE Sector, and preparation had to be started on the 27th.	
	30		The transport of No.2 Section joined 4th Bay now, to move by road to new area. Remainder of No.2 Section, and No.3 Section joined their Brigades, to march and entrain to new area.	
			As the Division was to assume command of new sector on 3rd December, the communications were reconnoitred, and personnel sent forward to commence relief.	

J. Grange
Major O.C.
O.C. 14th Signal Co.

Vol 27

Confidential

War Diary
of the
14TH Signal Co R.E.

for December 1917.

Volume 31

Army Form C. 2118.

WAR DIARY
of
INTELLIGENCE SUMMARY.
(Erase heading not required.)

Instructions regarding War Diaries and Intelligence Summaries are contained in F. S. Regs., Part II. and the Staff Manual respectively. Title pages will be prepared in manuscript.

Place	Date	Hour	Summary of Events and Information	Remarks and references to Appendices
WIZERNES	1st / 2nd / 3rd		Advance parties preceded by lorry. Transport by road and remainder of personnel by train to HQ Canal Bank YPRES. The Division took over Command of PASSCHENDAELE Sector noon 3rd Dec.	
	3rd onwards		The Division was in this sector 24 days. The Division was disposed with one Bde in the line HQrs at GALLIPOLI (D.13.8.5) Belg Sheet 28 NE. One Bde in Support HQ at WIELTJE (C.28.d.8.8.) Belg Sheet 28 NW One Bde in reserve HQ at VLAMERTINGHE (H2 & 9.0.) Belg Sheet 28 NW BrigAd. Canal Bank (I.1.8.5) Belg Sheet 28 NW Climatic conditions were bad. The entire area forward of Bde H.Q. was impassable, except on roads, duck-board tracks owing to the mud. Old buried existed from DHQ to HQ Bde in support. These were gradually replaced by airline poled cable, as the hooks having been down about 12 months were very faulty. From Bde in Support to Bde in line a new bury	See line diagram attached No. I.

WAR DIARY

INTELLIGENCE SUMMARY

(Erase heading not required.)

existed which held fairly successfully. Forward of GATLI POLI (HQ Bde in the line) several buries were attempted. The regular depth was never obtained, owing to severe casualties to burying parties. Impossible conditions of mud existing. Consequently these buries were never through, having been irreparably dissed before they were even completed.

Loaded lines were then laid to Bns metallic circuits employed. This necessitated the use of D8 Cable with two coloured legs. Those who very difficult to obtain. Blue + yellows and green + yellows were found useful, but blue + green soon became indistinguishable in the mud.

More use might be made of this if the supplies of D8 with bi-coloured legs were available. D5 twisted was often issued in lieu for the forward work, was useless.

WAR DIARY

or

INTELLIGENCE SUMMARY

(Erase heading not required.)

Place	Date	Hour	Summary of Events and Information	Remarks and references to Appendices
			Visual Visual was most successful, froth was working up to BELLEVUE rights was obtained **Runners** Severe cas: nullie in these and in linemen were obtained owing to the very heavy continuous shelling **Power Buzzer Amplifier** Great attention was devoted to this. A squad of 2A men were attached from Battalions previously trained. Sets were set up in PASSCHENDAELE, MEETCHEELE and BELLEVUE. Great trouble was experienced in keeping these up. — in keeping base lines thro: in the carriage of accumulators, & in the reliefs of personnel, who were not sufficiently trained. Arrangements were made with this division to attach these permanently and better results are hoped for by this method	See Visual diagram attached No 2 See A+○ diagram attached No 2

WAR DIARY
INTELLIGENCE SUMMARY
(Erase heading not required)

Army Form C. 2118.

Place	Date	Hour	Summary of Events and Information	Remarks and references to Appendices
	3		W/T Sets. French Sets 50 watt DC were established. Similar trouble was experienced owing to, lack of training of personnel, aerials being shot away, and testing and supply of accumulators. A supernumerary officer was posted for W/T and matters were greatly improved by his arrival. The constant attention of one Officer to A. P.Bu3zc. MW/T only.	
	27th		The division was relieved on this day by 8th Division came back to WIZERNES, transport by road, remainder by train.	
	27th to 31st		No training was commenced. Xmas relax ations were allowed. Preparations for the move south to 5th Army. In area W of PERONNE were begun.	

R.M.eure
Captain R.E.
for O.C. 14th Signal Coy R.E.

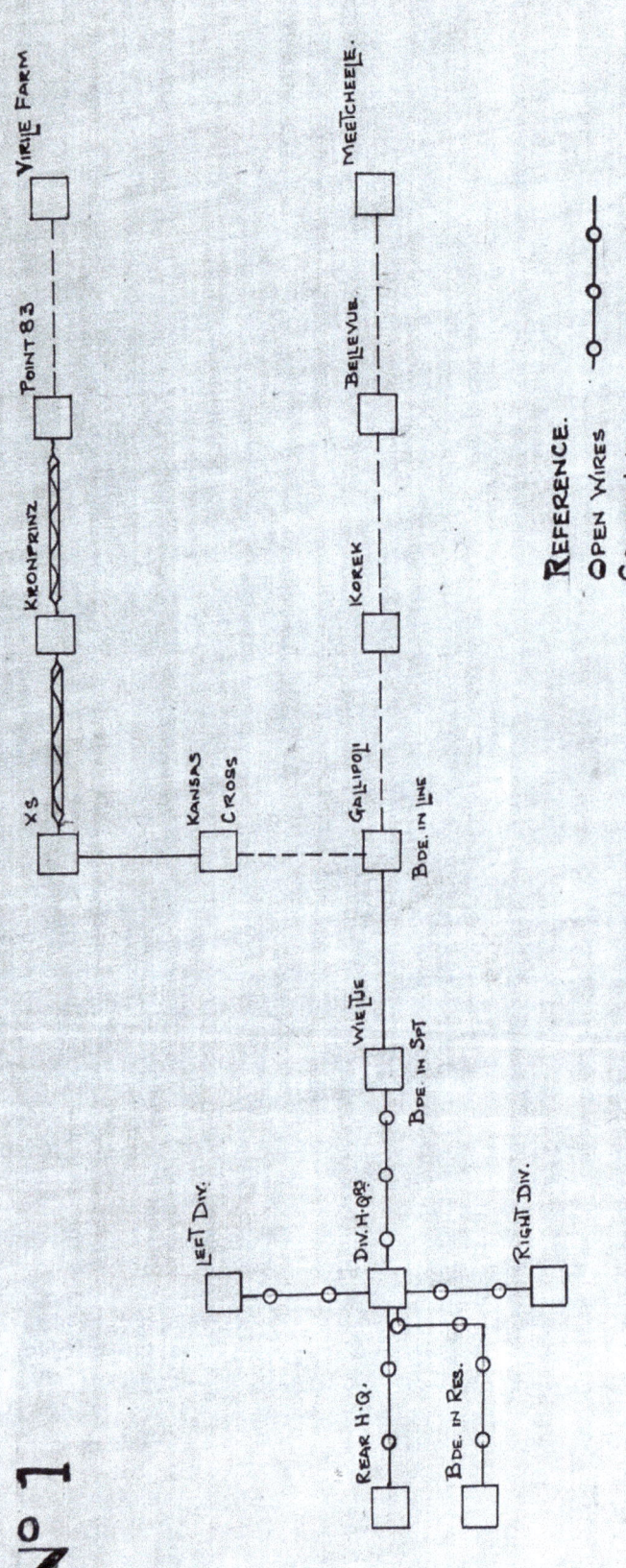

No 2

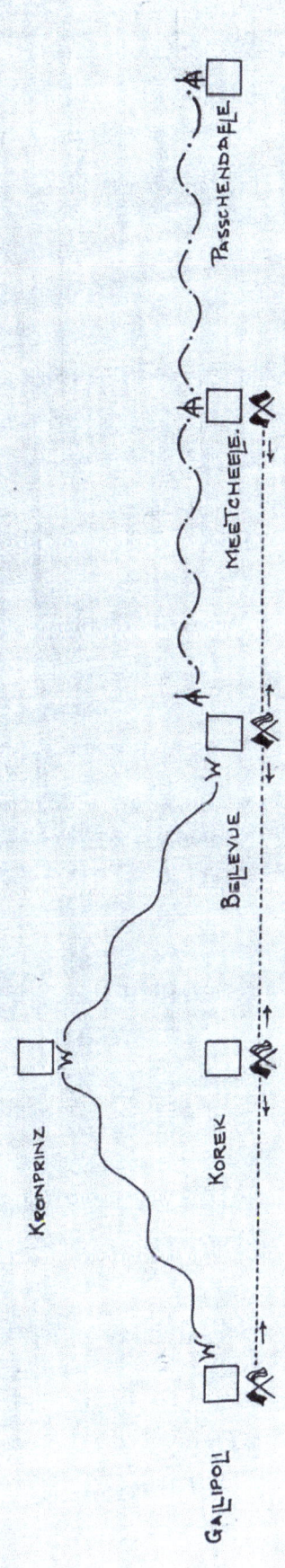

Reference.

Visual ·······
Power Buzzer —·—·—
& Amplifier }
Wireless ～～～

R.R. Weed
Capt. R.E.

14th SIGNAL COMPANY R.E.

Vol 28

Confidential

War Diary

of the

14th Signal Co. R.E.

From 1st January 1918   to 31st January 1918.

Volume 32

WAR DIARY
~~INTELLIGENCE SUMMARY~~

(Erase heading not required.)

Place	Date	Hour	Summary of Events and Information	Remarks and references to Appendices
WITERNES	2/1/8		Advance parties left for MERICOURT SUR SOMME by lorry.	
MERICOURT SUR SOMME	3/1/8		Signal Company marched to St OMER, and entrained for EDGEHILL where they detrained and marched to MERICOURT-SUR-SOMME	
			On arrival in this area, no communication to Brigades was available. A large number of old French routes were lying derelict in the area. (a back area of the Somme battlefield) Lines on these were regulated, joined through and where necessary salved cable was used. And training was certain derelict routes were salved, and training was embodied in the construction of new routes, with this material to replace cable. This proved very valuable, as it gave opportunity for the employment of French Air line stores. And also for testing French lines and learning French methods of revolution &/c.	

WAR DIARY
or
INTELLIGENCE SUMMARY.

(Erase heading not required.)

Army Form C. 2118.

Place	Date	Hour	Summary of Events and Information	Remarks and references to Appendices
MERICOURT SUR SOMME	22/8		The Signal Company moved by road to take over from the French Army. Advance parties were sent to Hd Qrs of 154th French Division to learn their routes & locality exchanges.	
GUISCARD	25/8		Signal Coy and Div Hd Qrs arrived in French back area at GUISCARD. A seperate exchange was opened with junctions to the French Exchange.	
CLASTRES	26/8		Signal Company moved to MONTESCOURT, and proceeded to open a fresh exchange at Hd Qrs of 154th French Division at CLASTRES. Brigade reliefs between English and French Brigades were carried out on night of 26/27th and 27/28th. Brigades remaining under French command. Division Hd Qrs. remaining at GUISCARD.	

WAR DIARY
INTELLIGENCE SUMMARY

(Erase heading not required.)

Army Form C. 2118.

Place	Date	Hour	Summary of Events and Information	Remarks and references to Appendices
	28/8		Seperate lines were put through to Bdes of Infantry and Artillery. In addition to the French lines in use, and brought on to an English exchange at CLASTRES Divisional Hd Qrs moved to CLASTRES. Communication was already passed to G.O.C 14th Division. In force to all Infantry and Artillery Bdes. French lines were put through during the day. From French Infantry HQrs to MONTES COURT to 14th Division Hd Qrs at CLASTRES and then alternate routes were ensured. French localiti exchanges were closed down and lines required strapped through	

WAR DIARY or INTELLIGENCE SUMMARY

Place	Date	Hour	Summary of Events and Information	Remarks and references to Appendices
	28/1/18		French pigeon lofts were taken over and pigeons used.	
	29/1/18		A new Signal Office was constructed and wires led in, and office was opened at 8 p.m. 29th Jany. The two having run concurrently till completion of the new Signal Office	
	30th		Work was done replacing old French locals, reeling them up, and improving existing French routes.	
	31st		Work was commenced by a 3rd Corps Cable Section, on joining French Div H.Q Ors at CLASTRES to French Infy and Arty HQ at MONTESCOURT, replacing and staying the most important route, that	

R.S Lindsay - Renton
Major
Cmdg 14th Divl Signal Coy RE

Vol 29

Confidential

War Diary

= of the =
14th Signal Coy R.E.

1st Feby 1918   to   28th Feby 1918.

(Volume 33.)

Army Form C. 2118.

WAR DIARY
or
INTELLIGENCE SUMMARY.
(Erase heading not required.)

Instructions regarding War Diaries and Intelligence Summaries are contained in F.S. Regs., Part II. and the Staff Manual respectively. Title pages will be prepared in manuscript.

Place	Date	Hour	Summary of Events and Information	Remarks and references to Appendices
CLASTRES	4th		All lines were led into Signal Office on "interruption" cable suspended from main terminal poles.	
	6th		All air lines were terminated one hundred to two hundred yards from Signal office, and buried in. All locals and bell wires were placed in a shallow bury, thus avoiding all overhead wires except P.E.L.'s likely to betray a headquarters.	
	8th to 28th		All three Brigade Headquarters were located in the line. Work commenced on main buried system to link up present headquarters of Brigades in line and also headquarters of Brigades, and Battalions in the Battle Zone, in the event of the Division retiring to this line. Three companies of infantry, approximate total 300, were detailed each day for this work. These numbers were not always obtained, owing to Battalion reliefs. The following method of digging, embodying a normal four hour task was found the best. First Day. 1 man dig a length of 7'6" to a depth of 4'. Second Day. 1 man deepen a length of 15' to a depth of from 4' to 6'. Third Day. 1 man fill in a length of 18'.	

WAR DIARY
or
INTELLIGENCE SUMMARY

(Erase heading not required.)

Army Form C. 2118.

Place	Date	Hour	Summary of Events and Information	Remarks and references to Appendices
	8th to 28th		It was found that this could be done in three and a half hours. Jack work of this description was found to be preferred by the infantry. All work was done in daylight, and thereby facilitated. No joints were buried, and manholes were made at every joint (every 440 yards), and the cable led into a bot, and jointed through. These were readily accessible, and had five feet to six feet cover, including channel iron, and log breakers, and afforded cover if necessary for two linesmen. Two large test points were made made at Le Fay Farm, and Cupola dug-outs. C.23.d.3.1. Work was also done repairing and re-regulating MONTESCOURT - REMIGNY route, the MONTESCOURT - JUSSY route, MONTESCOURT - CLASTRES road route. The buried route when complete was harrowed over in zig-zag lines to break its straight continuity.	See Appendix 1.

P.S. Hindley Renton
Major
O.C. 9/12th Signal Coy.

Army Form C. 2118.

WAR DIARY
or
INTELLIGENCE SUMMARY.

(Erase heading not required.)

Instructions regarding War Diaries and Intelligence Summaries are contained in F. S. Regs., Part II. and the Staff Manual respectively. Title pages will be prepared in manuscript.

Place	Date	Hour	Summary of Events and Information	Remarks and references to Appendices
APPENDIX I			Manhole Protected Joint Boxes	

PLAN.

TEST BOX
5' Cover.
3'0"
3'0"

Manhole
Trench Boards Ladder
A

C.I. Cover.
3'0"

Brick Rubble 2'0"
Earth 4'0"
Channel Iron
5'0"
Joint-Box
6"x8" Timbers
Corrugated Iron

Section on line AA.

14th Divisional Engineers

14th DIVISIONAL SIGNAL COMPANY R. E.

MARCH 1918

Army Form C. 2118.

14th Division Signal Coy R.E.

WAR DIARY
or
INTELLIGENCE SUMMARY.

(Erase heading not required.)

MARCH 1918

VOL 30

Instructions regarding War Diaries and Intelligence Summaries are contained in F. S. Regs., Part II. and the Staff Manual respectively. Title pages will be prepared in manuscript.

Place	Date	Hour	Summary of Events and Information	Remarks and references to Appendices
CLASTRES	March 1st		Board Route Continued	
"	2nd		Fay Farm – GIBERCOURT Commenced 79 men employed	
SAVY LE SEC	3rd		" " Continued 188 " "	
"	4th		" 238	
"	5th		" 162	
SEQUEHART	6th		" 240	
"	7th		" 235	
"	8th		" 257	
"	9th		" 230	
	10th		" 95	
	11th		LA SABLIERE ROUTE Commenced 164	
	12th		" 219	
	13th		FAY FARM – GIBERCOURT Route Completed 21	
			LA SABLIERE ROUTE Continued 263	
	14th		" 167	
	15th		" 158	
	16th		" 163	
			" 330	
			" 323	
	16th		Spur to 42nd Bn Fijis (Audregnies) 83	
			" 89	
	17th		LA SABLIERE ROUTE Continued 382	

Army Form C. 2118.

WAR DIARY
or
INTELLIGENCE SUMMARY.
(Erase heading not required)

Instructions regarding War Diaries and Intelligence Summaries are contained in F.S. Regs., Part II. and the Staff Manual respectively. Title pages will be prepared in manuscript.

Place	Date	Hour	Summary of Events and Information	Remarks and references to Appendices
CHARTRES Ref- Sheet 62 C.N.W.	1st		LA SABLIÈRE ROUTE (continued) 364 men employed	
			142 Rd Hyde Park Rgt Hqrs 151 " "	
			" " 95 " "	
			LA SABLIÈRE ROUTE (continued) 351 " "	
	2nd		Information received from Intelligence that prisoners report that O.C.'s on right & left O.C. Signals had G.S.O of Suffolks importance of completing LA SABLIÈRE ROUTE during to day. HA & R.E.'s O.R. on the left of light hearths by 14 pds on the Battle Zone. A.D.C. at present 1100 men allotted to repairs for work in the Z.F.	
			LA SABLIÈRE ROUTE completed 1400 cyds through Battle Zone. Main Battle Zone repaired & put in readiness day & dark. Main Battle Zone repaired	
		3.45 P.M.	G. Sgt Mens & pioneer men to E. Syph at LA SABLIERS taken part fully of 150 men to front of Huston flag total was finished at 4.30 P.M. 1100 of men employed.	
		4.4 A.M.	Enemy Commenced Heavy Bombardment of forward areas Hqrs including Qde Hqs. Hqs Staff H.Q.M.P.M.G. L H A.K. JOSSY which destroys Signal Office & all communications behind Bn Hqs. Wqds to Contwanty L P to rear this time Etsyonpront. He day. Communication with In the Regt I.F.O. to North Hingh Southwest by from this time Etsyonpront. He day. Bombardment down on Bde Hqs (and) which to Open in no letter this by H.Q of in Commencement of Bombs Regt Batt be terrible they remain in through All day. Horrible sectors top in Cable Bde Regt Bell Shot which loges within 30 yds of Bde Hqs. Owing to Barrage of gas Communication with these Bdes not through till about 4.15 P.M. when Bdes moved forward to Battle Zone	

Army Form C. 2118.

WAR DIARY
or
INTELLIGENCE SUMMARY.
(Erase heading not required.)

Instructions regarding War Diaries and Intelligence Summaries are contained in F. S. Regs., Part II. and the Staff Manual respectively. Title pages will be prepared in manuscript.

Place	Date	Hour	Summary of Events and Information	Remarks and references to Appendices
CLASTRES	March 21st	11 AM	Capt. Cobb detachment arrived communication trenches all manned through the whole of the day.	
Rd.			Pigeon message timed 10.20 am received from 62 Infants. 21 Inf.	
St 66 CAM			timed 11.40 am received from 42nd Inf. Bde HQrs	
St Quentin R		1p	Communication still direct with 118th Bn (Right Bn), + 36 4th Bn (Left Bn). 1a also	
			Communication still direct with 118th Bn (Right Bn) reported by 3rd 9th Bde	
			1C Alg. 3rd Corps.	
		12.46 PM	Pigeon Queen message from Shrapnel "EXCELLENT"	
			H20 D	
		1.30 PM	1.1 3rd Bde move HQrs to Shrapnel point	
			42nd Bde HQrs H.21.B. } Communication established about 4.15 PM	
		3.30 PM	43rd Bde H.25.a.62	
		9.15 PM	Division ordered to occupy Green Line Bindhyd PETIT DETROIT	
			4.1st Bn the NAVY 43rd Bde Hd Qrs. SAN DPT M26 D. 42nd Bde (Sgr. Robson) PETIT DETROIT	
			4.1 Bn the NAVY CLASTRES to PETIT DETROIT. Communicate with 41st	
	22nd	12 midnight	Division moved from CLASTRES to PETIT DETROIT. Bde & early in the morning to 43rd Bde arrived 4.15 Ack.	

WAR DIARY
INTELLIGENCE SUMMARY
(Erase heading not required.)

Army Form C. 2118.

Place	Date	Hour	Summary of Events and Information	Remarks and references to Appendices
PETIT DETROIT ST QUENTIN	22nd	1 PM	Sw Hqrs H.Q. moved from PETIT DETROIT to BEAUMONT EN BEINE. Communication with Wks at BOUCHOIR & 18th Div at UGNY & LE-BAY which they moved at 7AM from PO WEZ. Coy moved from UGNY - Le Bay at 12 P.M. Communication with 36th Inf Bde opened up at BEAUMONT. Coy moved up from CHASTRES.	
BEAUMONT EN ST QUENTIN			Owing to enemy advance all permanent lines to FLAVY exchange taken to ground and used for enemy lines to Bde telegraph. Communication to 143rd Bde via 12th Div 4 & 5 Infantry (Brit.) Yrs line communication to 143rd Bde 4.45 P.M. Communication to 143rd Bde thro Pts of the Cable Detachment to the Cable Detachment 4.45 P.M. Communication thro line 2 1/2 Rds. to North enemy W.T. failure after refunded thro pts of the Cable Detachment Runner lines from BEAUMONT Bde to the Quick Emerson Railway Exchange. Cable detachment Runner line to Advance to Battalion of permanent communication. Runners used for all emerg F.L.A.V.Y exchange owing to failure of permanent. Runners within ten miles outside F.L.A.V.Y exchange owing to falling of permanent line Brigade instead of the dark by laying off lines via Bde. Enemy started across the canal 4 1/2 - 6.43 W Bde Hqrs in neighbourhood of RIEZ-du-CUIGNY Communication to 143 Bde maintained & thro off 6.43 Bn HQrs put through.	
	23rd	12 noon	Div H.Q. moved from BEAUMONT EN BEINE to GUIVRY. Cable line laid by Cable Wagon via Canny to GUIVRY. Situation West of the Somme ? so next day station In the do no bright pullbrush Cavalry Bde & Spl Coys ? moved back it opening up Enemy fires moving forward again in position.	
GUIVRY St Quentin		1.15 PM	H.Q. 4th & 2nd (5th Bde moved from PETIT DETROIT to GUIVRY)	

Army Form C. 2118.

WAR DIARY
or
INTELLIGENCE SUMMARY.
(Erase heading not required)

Instructions regarding War Diaries and Intelligence Summaries are contained in F.S. Regs., Part II. and the Staff Manual respectively. Title pages will be prepared in manuscript.

Place	Date	Hour	Summary of Events and Information	Remarks and references to Appendices
GUIVRY	23rd March	4 PM	Gen'l Report Hqrs opened at GUIVRY. have been to Brow Brtdge. Communication to 5	
ST Quentin (?)			Gen'l of Division (G.H) at QUESMY. in a 3rd Corps.	
			Returned along tract to BEAUMONT now with sch established there 4/p 169th ORA FA	
			about this time. 42nd Bch moved to GUI (CAB) Response Sectors	
	24th	10.40 am	14th Division ordered to form up at F.M de FRANDES. BEINES WIA 2.0. DADG tent w/off	
			Office communication arranged. Incidents from BEAUMONT	
QUESMY		11 AM	Div HQ moved from GUIVRY to QUESMY. Communication to Corps at NOYON. Infantry personnel	
A paration/a			in touch of gun. Enemy to touch. Retiring along available rd. Communication to FT 188 F (443) 58	
			BEINES DAD Surrendered Tank BOUCHOIRE & GUIVRY. Units in contact to touch BRAND EG BEINES	
			turn to G touch Div in QUESMY Chateau	
			14 Div Artillery Commanded at CROIXET	
CRISOLLES		5.35 pm	Div Hqrs move from QUESMY to CRISOLLES. Division Low Artillery Command with of NOYON	
France ?				
LAGNY		8 PM	Div HQ moved to LAGNY. Division retired to take up position west side of NOYON	
France ?		12 PM	CANAL Comm'g moved at HAUDIVAL & BEAURAINS	
			Communication with 3rd Corps via French Car Corps at LAGNY & thence thro' French Corps at NOYON	

Army Form C. 2118.

WAR DIARY
or
INTELLIGENCE SUMMARY.

(Erase heading not required.)

Instructions regarding War Diaries and Intelligence Summaries are contained in F.S. Regs., Part II. and the Staff Manual respectively. Title pages will be prepared in manuscript.

Place	Date	Hour	Summary of Events and Information	Remarks and references to Appendices
LASSIGNY then to CHIRY then to PIMPREZ 17	25th	9AM	Divn H/Q moved to CHIRY. Communication opened to Corps & pneumatic tube. Communication only possible by R.S.O. Rn. R.O. & 200 H/ps during Advance	
		6.30pm	Divn move to Divn LEFRANC forbin. Recce reported returning to N of the Canal.	
		12.5am & onwards	Enemy patrols repulsed - 61 yon during night. Bridges to N of THIESCOURT	
	26th	3AM	Divn H/Q moved from CHIRY to point about ½ mile between CHIRY and RIBERCOURT. Divn Drus Transport hd side of road not far. Transports remainder of Div'n moved	
			Communication when Divn Drs Transport halted Ready. LATEN OUT. Corps H/Q also here	
RIBERCOURT Pimprez 17	26th	5.30AM	Divn H/Q moved to RIBERCOURT.	
		7AM	Orders received Brigades to concentrate at L'ECOUILLON	
		10PM	Cable detachment sent off to CHATEAU de RIMBERLIEU in VILLERS-sur-COUDUN for Cou Dun to lay lines to Bdes	
			Assembly place at ELINCOURT close VILLER-sur-COUDUN	
VILLERS-sur-COUDUN		5PM	Divn H.Q. closed at RIBERCOURT & opened at CHÂTEAU de RIMBERLIEU which were in same village. On duty under French Commun cab'in to Corps via Corps Itonio. 1 Cable detachment - sent to A.H.Btty	
			at CHEVINCOURT communication via Corps Itonio	
ESTRÉES ST. DENIS SOLENTE BEAUVAIS 21	27th	12.30 PM	Divn (with A.H.Btty) moved to ESTRÉE ST. DENIS. Communication with Corps via French Exchange in village. + COMPIÈGNE.	

Army Form C. 2118.

WAR DIARY
or
INTELLIGENCE SUMMARY

(Erase heading not required.)

Instructions regarding War Diaries and Intelligence Summaries are contained in F. S. Regs., Part II. and the Staff Manual respectively. Title pages will be prepared in manuscript.

Place	Date	Hour	Summary of Events and Information	Remarks and references to Appendices
ESTREE-ST DENIS BEAUVAIS	March 28th	1.15	Division ordered to move to the PONT SUR MAXENCE area.	
SARRON		9 PM	Division stopped at CHATEAU VILETTE (SARRON) Communication through French civil exchange to GHQ very difficult	
BEAUVAIS	March 29th	9 AM	Division ordered to move by bus from GHQ to 5th Army area. Advanced HQrs moved to HEBECOURT during afternoon	
HEBECOURT AMIENS	March 30th		Division in Telephonic Communication with 5th ARMY at DURY. Divisional HQrs then transferred awhile to LOEUILLY.	

Army Form C. 2118.

WAR DIARY
INTELLIGENCE SUMMARY.
(Erase heading not required)

Instructions regarding War Diaries and Intelligence Summaries are contained in F. S. Regs., Part II. and the Staff Manual respectively. Title pages will be prepared in manuscript.

Place	Date	Hour	Summary of Events and Information	Remarks and references to Appendices
			NOTES on Communications Period of Operations March 21st March 26th After the 21st the fighting developed into open warfare the following points are thought to warrant the object of drawing attention to the problems that arose. I. Communications. (A) CORPS All lines to my Command had to be arranged by this Command. During the operations of March 23rd all communication laterally had to be arranged by this Command, in the most efficient and cheapest manner. Artillery ie the Wireless of B Field was always situated involved employing the continuous moving and laying of lines which was practically impracticable (B) BRIGADES All wireless of the Brigade zone command station was abandoned fairly soon and trouble of signalling to Brigades was felt. It was difficult to know of wireless where the battn was. This period entirely satisfactory. Owing to lack of portability it was not found possible to use H.P. set after the moving of the next day or so in cases were always of use to us that down. (C) BRIGADE to BATTNS. Chiefly runners and visual, of the telephony owing to loss of equipment drawbacks. (D) Flanking Divisions Frequently S.O.S. rockets when they did occur in coop to the locality. This considered that at many of them H.P. stood at some immediately brightly by top of rockets showed possible continued. In spite of many difficulties which has to mostly occurred all the items to the Division at once. During the whole time the Division was much at COMPIEGNE the Brigade works remained through with the troops of a Second location of a forward section to have a Brigade "on an important R.P.I. Road stretch of the forward and there turns were able to reach B.6. depot or certain a few head of the lines of areas etc.	

(A3092) Wt W28539/M1293 75,000 1/17 D.D. & L., Ltd. Forms/C.2118/14.

Army Form C. 2118.

WAR DIARY
or
INTELLIGENCE SUMMARY.
(Erase heading not required.)

Instructions regarding War Diaries and Intelligence Summaries are contained in F. S. Regs., Part II. and the Staff Manual respectively. Title pages will be prepared in manuscript.

Place	Date	Hour	Summary of Events and Information	Remarks and references to Appendices

II. Moves.

A. Staff &c.

It was always found that transport should have reached its move as a unit under an officer & carts detachments. Apart from units subjected to this transport. This always seem would not have had DHQ & WHQ moved. He has appealed to open officers men and advance parts of data & a staff in which has occasionally obtained from the Commander to bring work that transport with its being in signal War. The remainder of officer personal will move accordingly. Near this transport in on the day by the Horse Dir Reft on the lorries supplied by our MT Coy. Type 3 Ton lorry in charge of this unit was not of action in playing for almost seven, situating the allotted lying down they hung no means of getting around, but G F of L being was out of action at the 3 lorries [illegible] seven which the crew felt about April 20th.

B. Units from the point of view of communication.

It was found that the point of system was to have an advanced office style. When two teams office advanced steadily out till the very last moment until that all communications nearly. Who its which there was to ponder. It was constantly difficult to find out like the Sig that movement actual positions were. Its most of the formation is known when they were held up & whether very unsatisfactory. All units must move from the next hourer formation & constantly unable to be kept when they reach their new move are apt if this is the cause of the delay in communication failing breakdown between them. The operation orders Cannot & in only be kept in reserve if this is to be the place / resilience for their style the operation orders. Sometimes orders to join forward orders were not sufficiently

---

III. STORES.

The conditions relatively [illegible] must of obvious distinction classes of stores employed by Divas. Tpt.
[illegible] should be employed [illegible] All Divisional MT Draw [illegible] stores should be attached by Pet to A general supply.
For Wiring &c should [illegible] the units that [illegible] When only they tops for transporter to Army of Divisional Signals. N.1 wagons should store in hire battle is the inappropriateness should be allowed for this type of Division stores to include wire when his [illegible] be of too lower battles it seem & have inappropriate as shown for this type of Division Signal office stores which is as it was officers rapidly type this without delay & large amount of that was also required in the Divisional Signal office equipment was carried. Small portable tables of [illegible] fell from tree Pelhams to be shortl to an inconv. On the long traffic I mentioned, Quite a short which mould both while to carry all dues about what could be carried without loss of portable. Its found of other stories. It is hoped will assist while to carry all the duties by that absorb [illegible] Stores notion [illegible] be the possession of the stores distribution of motor cycles to as DTR

WAR DIARY
or
INTELLIGENCE SUMMARY.
(Erase heading not required.)

Army Form C. 2118.

Instructions regarding War Diaries and Intelligence Summaries are contained in F. S. Regs., Part II. and the Staff Manual respectively. Title pages will be prepared in manuscript.

Place	Date	Hour	Summary of Events and Information	Remarks and references to Appendices
STEENWERCK (contd)			So all our base details, on the lines of the French Intendance convoys, would contain necessary personnel to hand, would have been available for the movement of M.T. much later not Bdes. Moreover would [any type] of the [Product] or other [Mobile] H.Qrs. during these operations. The [portable] masts etc. should be embodied in the [details].	
TRANSPORT			This by was without 6 Sp. of Cars from about a week after operations commenced until about the 16th of April. The difficulties of running communication & survey operations of this kind without a car can only be fully realised by those who have done it. The [cars] missing [but by] Dn M.T. [way 3] [ ] be repair[ed] [ ] of [action]. Should the [situation as] regards getting stores [fast] [ ] [ ] only 4 h.p. [cycles] were [kept] [ ] [ ] [ ] [by] [ ] [ ] [ ] [ ] [ ] [ ] [ ] breakdown. The replacement of [horses] was [ ] [ ] [ ] [by] [ ] [ ] [ ] [ ] being [numerous]. It is considered that the establishment of a D.R. L.S. of Brigades [ ] L.Corps should be increased to at least 22. This should allow of 2 h. each Bde. 3 to Dn. Dty to [keep] [at] least 13 including 10 t. Sp. [ ] which [ ] had such Cars as these to [ ] [ ] [ ] during the time. Should of the [ ] [ ] a line of H.Q. [ ] [ ] [ ] [ ] of ours [ ] [ ] in [mobile] warfare. The present system of [obtaining] Signal Transport [ ] [ ] [ ] very unsatisfactory & it is suggested that the placement of Sp. all transport ought to be done directly by D.S.[ ] [ ] Army with D.D.S.T. Army.	

R.S. Lindsay-Renton
Major
Cmdg 14th Division Signal Coy R.E.

WAR DIARY

14th DIVISIONAL SIGNAL COMPANY.

A P R I L

1 9 1 8

Army Form C. 2118.

WAR DIARY
or
INTELLIGENCE SUMMARY
(Erase heading not required.)

APRIL 1918

Place	Date April	Hour	Summary of Events and Information	Remarks and references to Appendices
BOVES (Amiens 17)	1st		Division relieved 20th Division and 2nd Cavalry Division, in the line south of VILLERS BRETTONNEUX. Div HQ (rear) at BOVES, connected by airline to Corps. Locality Exchange in the same village. Cable and airline routes picked up to Advanced Div. HQ at cross roads due east of St Nicolas. Lines laid out to Brigades, before their arrival and men left at Brigade ends to lead in when Brigade HQ were fixed.	
	2nd		No communication with 43rd Bde was obtained till 6.0 am owing to them not going to the H.Q. ordered. Division was relieved by French troops, during the evening as the French Division was stronger, their disposition was different and no communications were handed over. Owing to entraining of Division, transport had not arrived so 19th Corps ran S.S. Cable Section. to 14th Division.	
AUBIGNY	3rd		Division relieved 1st Cavalry Division, and 16th Division in line from Somme southwards. Reinforced HQ at AUBIGNY, and temporary report centre at FOUILLOY. Airline picked up to Corps, from AUBIGNY, and FOUILLOY. Speid at AUBIGNY. Cable route to FOUILLOY ground cable to Brigades, taken over from 1st Cavalry Division.	
	4th	5.15 am	Enemy attacked. The report centre at FOUILLOY decided to remain, but changed to a place 600 yards away consequent confusion of lines	

Army Form C. 2118.

WAR DIARY
or
INTELLIGENCE SUMMARY

APRIL 1918

(Erase heading not required.)

Instructions regarding War Diaries and Intelligence Summaries are contained in F. S. Regs., Part II. and the Staff Manual respectively. Title Pages will be prepared in manuscript.

Place	Date April	Hour	Summary of Events and Information	Remarks and references to Appendices
AUBIGNY (contd)	4		FOUILLOY was being shelled, & communication was lost to Brigades & Corps, from FOUILLOY.	
FOUILLOY		6.30 a	Aeroplanes terminated in FOUILLOY and communication backward restored. New office opened in School.	
		9.0 am	Loose wagon laid line to 413 Bde, communication successfully established	
		11.0 am	" " " " 143 " "	
		1.0 pm	Cable detachments of the 14 Division arrived	
		2.0 p	Australian Bde of 5 Australian Division moved into line, taking over our left flank, communication established with them by cable wagon.	
GUISY	5		Division relieved during the night by 5th Australian Divn & 2 Cav. Div. and came into reserve on the line behind AUBIGNY. Divisional H.Q. at GUISY. Permanent and railway route picked up, to Corps and cable wagons laid to 141 & 143 Bdes. No lines were laid to 142 Bde, the majority of the Headquarters having been captured.	
ST. FUSCIEN	7		Division moved into reserve at ST. FUSCIEN. Communication via Corps Heavies Ex in the village	

Army Form C. 2118.

WAR DIARY or INTELLIGENCE SUMMARY

(Erase heading not required.)

APRIL 1918

Place	Date	Hour	Summary of Events and Information	Remarks and references to Appendices
ST FUSCIEN	9		Transport moved off by road, taking two days march to FEQUIERES	
	10		Remainder marched by road to SALEUX Entrained for GAMACHES, detrained and marched to FEQUIERES	
	11		Company and transport entrained at FEQUIERES	
	12	1.40 a.	Detrained at H.Q. of MARESQUES & marched by road to HUCQUELIERS arriving at two p.m.	
HUCQUELIERS	14		H3 Bde organised as a composite Bde. of 4 Battalions. Signal section made remaining complete with men, & stores held by HQ section. Stores were now very low as all Brigades & Battalions came out without any stores, and those in possession of Headquarters were only what the two lorries had been able to carry, being constantly loaded.	
	15		H1 & H2 Bde Troops sent to H3 Bde to form composite Brigade. Headquarters moved to Laires area.	
ECQUEDECQUES			Sig HQ moved to ECQUEDECQUES, accompanied by sufficient number of Signal company to man HQ office. Remainder of Company moved to LAIRES area where training was commenced	
LAIRES	16		Before 21st March 19 men of the Royal Sussex Regt were sent from Base for	

Army Form C. 2118.

WAR DIARY
or
INTELLIGENCE SUMMARY

(Erase heading not required.)

APRIL 1918

Place	Date	Hour	Summary of Events and Information	Remarks and references to Appendices
LAIRES	16		Transferred to No. 5 Section. On construction of Buried routes 30 signallers from disbanded Battalions were lent to assist 16 men were also held as Divisional Power Buzzer and Amplifier Section. Ten Signallers from Rouen Battalion were also held for arrival, as there were considerable casualties	

Major
Cmdg 1st Signal Con RE.

Army Form C. 2118.

WAR DIARY
or
INTELLIGENCE SUMMARY

(Erase heading not required.) April 17-30

Instructions regarding War Diaries and Intelligence Summaries are contained in F.S. Regs., Part II. and the Staff Manual respectively. Title Pages will be prepared in manuscript.

Place	Date	Hour	Summary of Events and Information	Remarks and references to Appendices
LAIRES	17/18		Company training	
WANDERCOURT	19		Company moved to WANDERCOURT	
FRESSIN	21		" " " FRESSIN	
			Div HQ moved from ECQUEDECQUES to COYECQUE. Drop office left at ECQUEDECQUES to dispose of traffic to RE units	
			Company joined Div HQ	
COYECQUE	22		W.H.B. takes proceeded to S/d Div Signal Coy. as O/c W/T.	
	23		Infantry signallers attached from R. Sussex, & K.O.Y.L.I. tested with view to transfer to RE to form No 5 Section	
	24		Company training, cable and driving drill.	
	25/27		Rd Gilbert proceeded to 46 Bde REA Signal Sub Section as O/c.	
	28		Div Power Buzzer and Amplifier Section returned to Base	
			Div HQ moved to MOLINGHEM, with sufficient men of Signal Coy to man Div Signal office under Ed Fox.	
	30		Company moved to KEBIEZ. New office at TORCY, dealing with traffic for Brigades, and administrative services. Located in TORCY and FRUGES AREA	

CONFIDENTIAL

War Diary

of the

14th Divisional Signal Coy. R.E.

For May 1918

Volume 36

WAR DIARY or INTELLIGENCE SUMMARY

Army Form C. 2118.

May 1918.

Place	Date	Hour	Summary of Events and Information	Remarks and references to Appendices
LEBIEZ	1		Courses and Sounder working commenced for HQ and soft Section. N°1 Section. Cable and driving drill.	
	3		Class for Infantry Signal Officers commenced under Lt S.L. Deane. Airline route to FRESSIN dismantled	
	6		One dismounted cable detachment lent to XI Corps for airline work.	
	8		Air HQ moved from MOLINGHEM to ST QUENTIN leaving drop office at MOLINGHEM to deal with 2 field companys and Portuguese Brigade. Rear office moved from TORCY to LEBIEZ	
	10		A+Q leaving joined the Division at ST QUENTIN. Scheme carried out by Coy under Capt E.E. Reut M.C.	
	11		1 cable detachment proceeded to work under 14th Div. Artillery. Lt Bradford 8th KRRC took over Officers Signal Class	
	12		Company moved to MOULIN LE COMTE staying night at LAIRES. Officers Signal Class and rest office remaining at LEBIEZ.	
MOULIN LE COMTE	13		Party of 25 men under Lts Trimble and Hobson proceeded to work under XIII Corps on Airline system	
	15		41st Bde moved to AIRE	
	17		" " " BOISEGHEM	
	18		Major L.S Linsey Renton M.C left for ABBEVILLE	
	22		42 Bde moved to ROYON. 43. to TORCY.	
	24		Parties from XI & XIII Corps rejoined Coy.	

Army Form C. 2118.

WAR DIARY
or
INTELLIGENCE SUMMARY

(Erase heading not required.)

Instructions regarding War Diaries and Intelligence Summaries are contained in F.S. Regs., Part II. and the Staff Manual respectively. Title Pages will be prepared in manuscript.

Place	Date	Hour	Summary of Events and Information	Remarks and references to Appendices
MOULIN LE COMTE	MAY 26		Telegraphic and Telephonic day throughout XI Corps.	
	28		Capt F.E. Read M.C. conducted a skeleton scheme with the 1st Portuguese Division.	
	31		Capt F.E. Read M.C. left to command "R" Corps Signal Company.	

Confidential

WAR DIARY
— of the —
14th Signal Coy R.E.

June 1918

Volume 37

Army Form C. 2118.

WAR DIARY
or
INTELLIGENCE SUMMARY
(Erase heading not required.)

JUNE 1-7

Instructions regarding War Diaries and Intelligence Summaries are contained in F.S. Regs., Part II. and the Staff Manual respectively. Title Pages will be prepared in manuscript.

Place	Date JUNE	Hour	Summary of Events and Information	Remarks and references to Appendices
MOULIN LE COMTE	1		L. A. H. G. Coy M.C. left for temporary duty at Signal Depot.	
	2		1st Division transferred from XJ to X Corps.	
	3		"	
	4		43rd Inf Bde moved to FONTES	
	5		Officers Signal Class dispersed, and rear office closed down at TORCY.	
	6		Routine work	
	7		" "	

2449 Wt. W14957/M90 750,000 1/16 J.B.C. & A. Forms/C.2118/12.

Army Form C. 2118.

WAR DIARY
or
INTELLIGENCE SUMMARY
(Erase heading not required.)

JUNE 1—7

Place	Date	Hour	Summary of Events and Information	Remarks and references to Appendices
MOULIN LE COMTE	JUNE 1		Lt. A.M.G. Cox M.C. left for temporary duty at Signal Depot.	
	2		14th Division transferred from XI to X Corps.	
	3		43rd Inf. Bde moved to FONTES.	
	4		Officers Signal Class dispersed, and rear office closed down at TORCY.	
	5		Routine work	
	6		" "	
	7			

WAR DIARY
~~INTELLIGENCE SUMMARY.~~
(Erase heading not required.)

Army Form C. 2118.

Place	Date	Hour	Summary of Events and Information	Remarks and references to Appendices
MOULIN LE COMTE	8/6/18		Capt H. TREPESS R.E. reported from 18th Divl Artillery Signals as 2nd in Command 14th Divl Signal Co R.E.	
"	9/6/18		Routine work. Class commenced for No 5 Section in general signal duties. Capt L.R. THODAY M.C. 6th NORTH STAFFS REGT T.F. reported from Signal Sect AUSTRALIAN CORPS H.A. as OC. 14th Divl SIGNAL Co R.E.	K
"	10/6/18		Routine work. O.C. and 2nd i/command visited Bde Sections. 41 Bde No 2 Sect BOESEGHEM. 42 Bde No 3 Sect LA LACQUE, 43 Bde No 4 Sect FONTES.	K
"	11/6/18 } 12/6/18 } 13/6/18 } 14/6/18 }		Routine work continued	K
"	15/6/18		Scheme of Signal Communications for Defence of the LILLERS-STEENBECQUE line sent in to 14th Divl "G"	K copy attached
"	16/6/18		Divl H.Qrs and Staff of Int Bdes left for ENGLAND. Line laid from MOLINGHEM exchange to L'OBLOIS WOOD for 5th Command't Rufn	K
"	17/6/18		Nos 3 and 4 Sections marched into MOULIN LE COMTE.	K

WAR DIARY
~~INTELLIGENCE SUMMARY~~

(Erase heading not required.)

Army Form C. 2118.

Place	Date	Hour	Summary of Events and Information	Remarks and references to Appendices
MOULIN LECOMTE	18/6/18		Routine work. Power Buzzer Class commenced for men of Nos 3, 4 and 5 Section under 2/Lieut G.E. HOBSON RE. Eight men of Ree Section joined No 5 Sect class.	
"	19/6/18		Routine work & as above	K
"	20/6/18		LIEUT A. MACLEOD RE reported from Signal Sect AUSTRALIAN CORPS as OC No 1B Section.	K
"	21/6/18		MOLINGHEM and ECQUEDECQUES exchanges closed. BOESEGHEM exchange left open and manned by No 2 Section. No 2 Sect kept at BOESEGHEM on account of sickness	K
"	22/6/18		Routine work	K
"	23/6/18		Lt St. DEANE OC No 3 Sect proceeded on 3 weeks Wireless Course to 1st Army Signal School.	K
"	24/6/18		Power Buzzer class abandoned owing to sickness in the Coy.	K
"	25/6/18		Routine work	K
"	26/6/18		No 5 Sect class abandoned owing to sickness.	K
"	27/6/18		Routine work	K

Army Form C. 2118.

WAR DIARY
or
INTELLIGENCE SUMMARY.
(Erase heading not required.)

Instructions regarding War Diaries and Intelligence Summaries are contained in F. S. Regs., Part II. and the Staff Manual respectively. Title pages will be prepared in manuscript.

Place	Date	Hour	Summary of Events and Information	Remarks and references to Appendices
MOULIN LE COMTE	28/6/18		Routine work	15
"	29/6/18		"	15
"	30/6/18		"	15
			30/6/18	
			Murray Major.	
			OC 14 Divl Signal Coy RE.	

SECRET

H.Q. 14th (Light) Division, G.

Attached is scheme of communications for the defence of the LILLERS - STEENBECQUE Line.

Brigade to Battalion schemes will be forwarded as soon as completed.

[signature]

Captain,
O.C. 14th Div. Signal Coy.

14/6/1918

S E C R E T
****

14th (LIGHT) DIVISION

SCHEME OF COMMUNICATION FOR THE MANNING OF THE
LILLERS - STEENBECQUE Line.

Ref. Map. Sheet 36A 1/40,000.

Div.H.Q. - Infantry Bdes.
----

1. GENERAL.

Communications at present in use would remain.

It is proposed to supplement these by four cable routes, from Divisional H.Q. to Brigades.

These routes would be laid immediately orders were received to "Man Battle Stations."

They have been already reconnoitred by the Officers and men who would lay the lines, and obstacles which would delay progress have already been overcome, so that no time would be wasted in getting these lines laid.

2. PRESENT COMMUNICATIONS.
   (In black on attached diagram.)

(a). 14th Div. - 43rd Inf.Bde. Right Sector. FONTES.
   Open wires throughout via AIRE exchange and 1st Canadian Div. Exchange at FONTES.

(b). 14th Div. - 42nd Inf.Bde. Centre Sector, LA LACQUE.
   Cable to AIRE exchange, open wires AIRE to LA LACQUE.

(c). 14th Div. - 41st Inf.Bde. Left Sector. BOESEGHEM.
   Open wires to AIRE and THIENNES Cable THIENNES to BOESEGHEM.

(d). 14th Div. - ECQUEDECQUES exchange, for British Mission attached 2nd Portuguese Infantry Brigade. Open wires ST.QUENTIN - AUCHY AU BOIS - ECQUEDECQUES.

(e). 14th Div. - MOLINGHEM exchange for 61st Division adv. 61st Field Coy. Open wires via LAMBRES.

3. ROUTES TO BE LAID TO SUPPLEMENT EXISTING LINES.
   (In red on attached diagram)

(a). 14th Div. - 43rd Inf.Bde. Right Sector, FONTES.
   Route. ST.QUENTIN - ST.ANDRE FARM - N 9 b 3.8 7 -
   N 15 b 8.4 - Quarries in N 21 a - ROMBLY - FONTES.

(b). 14th Div. - 42nd Inf.Bde. Centre Sector, LA LACQUE.
   Route. ST.QUENTIN - Drill ground in H 33 b - MISSISSIPPI
   - H 36 a 7.1 - LA LACQUE.

(c). 14th Div. - 41st Inf.Bde. Left Sector, BOESEGHEM.
Route. ST.QUENTIN - MOULIN LE COMTE - RINCQ -
CENSE A L'AVOINE in H 15 central - GUARLINGHEM,
Canal crossing at H 11 central - I 13 & 1.4 -
BOESEGHEM.

(d). 14th Div. - ECQUEDECQUES exchange.
For British Mission and 2nd Portuguese Inf.Bde.
Route. Existing open wires to AUCHY AU BOIS
Cable to T 16 b 5.9 - T 11 d - T 12 c 9.1 - through
U 13 b to ECQUEDECQUES.

NOTE. It is not proposed to supplement the present line to MOLINGHEM.

4. D. R. L. S.

D.Rs. would run three times daily, over routes previously reconnoitred, starting from Div. H.Q. at 7 a.m. 2 p.m. and 8 p.m.

Run I.	Run II.	Run III.
Div. H.Q.	Div. H.Q.	Div. H.Q.
43rd Bde. FONTES	42nd Bde. LA LACQUE	41st Bde. BOESEGHEM.
ECQUEDECQUES	Div. H.Q.	Div. H.Q.
43rd Bde.		
Div. H.Q.		

5. TIME.

Time would be sent to all Brigades daily at 9.15 a.m., and at other times as required by the Staff.

6. As soon as possible, i.e. stores being available, and the tactical situation permitting, a second cable line would be run to each Infantry Brigade from Div.H.Q. for telegraphic purposes.

7. WIRELESS.

Three trench sets are being supplied. These would be situated at or near to each Infantry Bde. H.Q. and would work in conjunction with the Wilson set at Div. H.Q.
O.C. Wireless will arrange for wave lengths and calls.

8. VISUAL.

Visual communication will be arranged as follows :-

Div. H.Q. Station ST.QUENTIN Church.
Transmitting station at N 15 d 80.05.
From this transmitting station, visual can be obtained with FONTES church tower for 43rd Infantry Bde.
LA LACQUE 42nd Inf.Bde.
BOESEGHEM 41st Inf.Bde.

It is not proposed to man these stations unless absolutely necessary, as probably, with Wireless and despatch riders, messages would get through more quickly than by visual.

9. AEROPLANE DROPPING GROUNDS.

* It is proposed to arrange two aeroplane dropping grounds,
One near Div. H.Q.
One for Artillery, to be arranged when batteries get into position.

10. INF.BDES. TO BATTALIONS.

Copies of Bde. Schemes will be forwarded as soon as they are completed.

Appendices will be issued dealing with -

    (a). Pigeons.
    (b). Power buzzer and amplifier.
    (c). Message carrying rockets,

As soon as the arrangements regarding the supply of these additional means of communication are known.

No messenger dogs would be available.

These means of communication would be used to supplement any telephonic or runner communications between Battalions and Companies.

CONFIDENTIAL

War Diary.

— of the —

14th Signal Coy R.E.

1st July 1918 ———— 31st July 1918.

(Volume 34)

WAR DIARY
or
INTELLIGENCE SUMMARY.
(Erase heading not required.)

Army Form C. 2118.

Place	Date	Hour	Summary of Events and Information	Remarks and references to Appendices
			/4 DIVL SIGNAL Co RE. JULY 1918.	
MOULIN LE CONTE	1/7/18		Routine work	K
"	2/7/18		do.	K
"	3/7/18		Divl Details came under II Army from noon	K
"	4/7/18		Routine work. Reported Company was hostile owing to men returning from hospital	K
"	5/7/18		Received orders from II Army to move on 6th to rejoin Divn at WIERRE EFFROY.	K
SETQUES	6/7/18		Company marched to SETQUES (13 miles) and billeted for night.	K
WIERRE EFFROY	7/7/18		Continued march to WIERRE EFFROY (23 miles) arriving there at 6.20pm. Bde section marched direct to their respective Bdes. Communication established with II Corps, all Bdes. M.G. Batt. Roads arranged and built when necessary by VII Corps. 2/L. RADBOURNE returns from leave	K
"	8/7/18		Division now under VII Corps 2nd Army. Cables laid to Pioneer Battn. No 5 Rest Camp. M.G. Batt. Div HQ WIERRE EFFROY. 41 I Bde HARDINGHEN. 43 I Bde BOURSIN. 42 I Bde SOUVERAIN MOULIN. M.G. Batt. LA MALOTERIE. Pioneer Battn. REBERTINGUE	K

Army Form C. 2118.

WAR DIARY
or
INTELLIGENCE SUMMARY.
(Erase heading not required.)

Place	Date	Hour	Summary of Events and Information	Remarks and references to Appendices
WIERRE-EFFROY	8/7/18		Arrangements commenced for forming Divl Signal School for 200 untrained Battalion Signallers.	
"	9/7/18		Signal School arrangements temporarily postponed owing to probable move. D.D. Signals 2nd Army visited Company. A.D. Signals Training visited Coy & Signal School	
"	10/7/18		41 Bde moved from HARDINGHEN to LICQUES.	
"	11/7/18		1A Section moved to EPERLECQUES, also lorry with advanced office. 41 Bde moved from LICQUES to TOURNEHEM. 43 Bde moved from BOURSIN to LICQUES. 42 Bde moved from BAINCTHUN to BOURSIN.	
EPERLECQUES	12/7/18		Div HQRS moved to EPERLECQUES, 41 Bde SERQUES, 43 Bde GANSPETTE, 42 Bde TOURNEHEM.	
"	13/7/18		Arrangements recommenced for Divl Signal School - 100 men. Telephone communication completed to all Bdes, MG Batts. & Pnr Batt".	
"	14/7/18		Reconnoitred positions for HQrs of Divn and Bdes with G.S.O.I for defence of the WINNIZEELE line.	
"	15/7/18		Divl Signal School assembled at EPERLECQUES. Capt R.W NEWMAN Glouc Rgt O.C. Lt. S.L DEANE returned from 1st Army Wireless Course.	

WAR DIARY
or
INTELLIGENCE-SUMMARY.

(Erase heading not required.)

Army Form C. 2118.

Place	Date	Hour	Summary of Events and Information	Remarks and references to Appendices
EPERLECQUES	16/7/18		Classes commenced at Div Signal School. Visited WINNIZEELE area with G.O.C. and G.S.O.1 to decide Hqrs of Division and Bdes.	K
"	17/7/18		Routine work	K
"	18/7/18		A.D.Signals VII Corps visited Coy.	K
"	19/7/18		Visited WINNIZEELE. Communication with Capt PoPE VII Corps Signal, arranged for commencement of new route to Tuil Hqrs chosen.	K
"	20/7/18		Div Signal School moved to OUESTMONT, on account of XIX Corps School opening at EPERLECQUES Chateau. Church parades.	K
"	24/7/18			K
"	22/7/18		Visited WINNIZEELE Communication and Hqrs with Bde Signal Officers W/T Officer and Machine Gun Batt Signal Officer.	K
"	23/7/18		Provisional scheme of Communication for WINNIZEELE line completed	Copy attached
"	24/7/18		Divisional Signal School increased by 54 O.R.	K
"	25/7/18		Final scheme 43rd Inf Bde. Stations established at TOURNEHEM (BieltHqrs), WESTROVE, LA COMMUNAL and INGLINGHEM. Helio used during the greater part of the day.	K

Army Form C. 2118.

WAR DIARY
or
INTELLIGENCE SUMMARY.
(Erase heading not required.)

Instructions regarding War Diaries and Intelligence Summaries are contained in F. S. Regs., Part II. and the Staff Manual respectively. Title pages will be prepared in manuscript.

Place	Date	Hour	Summary of Events and Information	Remarks and references to Appendices
EPERLECQUES	26/7/18		Routine work.	15
"	27/7/18		Marching order parade of Hqrs & No 1 Section.	15
"	28/7/18		Church parade.	15
"	29/7/18		Routine work.	15
"	30/7/18		Inspection of Transport and Horse lines by G.O.C. 14 Division.	15
"	31/7/18		Routine work. Transport and horse lines moved into fresh field.	15

Ghoday. Major.
O.C. 14 Divl Signal Co. R.E.

31/7/18.

SECRET.

Arrangements for Signal Communications
WINNEZEELE Line.

Map Reference
  Sheet 27 1/40,000.

1.	On the Division occupying the WINNEZEELE Line, existing Communications as far as lines are concerned can be utilised to a large extent.

2.	The attached diagram shows existing buries, and proposed lines. Existing lines in GREEN, proposed in RED dotted. *NOT ATTACHED.*

3.	All the lines in existing buries would be at the disposal of the Division, and would be allotted to Brigades as required.

4.	Work has already been commenced on a trench running from Divisional H.Q. O.22.d.5.9 through the Centre Brigade H.Q. with a test box at O.24.b.5.0 to join up with main lateral bury at Test Point No. 7 about P.19.central.
	Another trench is under construction between BCP Test Point O.5.c.3.5 round the Northern side of CASSEL to join the main lateral bury at RECOLLETTE Test Point P.7.b.4.7.

5.	Test Boxes have been constructed at P.25.d.8.2 for the Right Brigade H.Q. P.26.c.3.6 and at J.31.c.5.1 for the Left Brigade H.Q. J.31.c.1.5.
	Cables would have to be laid between these Brigade H.Q. and their Test Boxes, distances of 250 yards and 300 yards respectively.

6.	In addition a cable would be laid from Divisional H.Q. round the rear of CASSEL hill, to join up with BCP Test Box O.5.c.3.5 thus giving an alternative route forward to the main lateral route. The route of this cable is shewn RED and GREEN dashes.

7. D.R.L.S.
   Divl. H.Q. to Right Bde.H.Q. and Centre Bde. H.Q.

	Via Railway Crossing in O.23.c., cross road in O.30.a.05.70 turn left to turning in O.24.a., turn right to Centre Bde.H.Q. on to cross roads P.19.a.8.5, turn right and straight down to Right Bde. H.Q.

   Divl. H.Q. to Left Bde. H.Q.

	Via BAVINCHOVE up CASSEL road to O.10.c.5.3 turn left up to O.9.b.9.9, turn left then right up track through O.3.c and b to O.3.b.90.75 to cross roads I.33.a.5.0 via L'ANGE to cross roads I.29.b.5.7, turn right through CROIX ROUGE, turn left to VERT VALLON, down track to right in I.36.d to Left Bde. H.Q.

8. VISUAL.

	The type of country lends itself well to Visual Communication and a number of Visual "Shots" have been tested. A plan of these has been sent to each Brigade Signal Officer. Full use should be made of these, as the existing buried lines only average 2'6" deep, and are consequently very liable to damage by shell fire.

9. WIRELESS.

As soon as practicable Wireless Communication would be established between Division and Brigades.

Power Buzzers would be issued to Brigades for forward work as soon as they became available. The use of Power Buzzers and loop sets would depend largely on the number of men trained in their use, available at the time. Brigade Signal Officers will reconnoitre Power Buzzer Bases as early as possible.

10. A <u>small</u> reserve of cable would be available, but as this would be very limited, economy in laying lines would be most essential.

11. As soon as Battalion Headquarters are fixed, Brigade Signal Officers will draw up schemes for communication with them

    (a) By the existing routes.
    (b) By laying cable, amount required to be stated.
    (c) By Runner, Cyclist, Mounted Orderly, Showing routes

12. Other means of communication in the forward area e.g. Rockets, Pigeons, Dogs &c., will be arranged as soon as the available supply is known.

Major,
O.C. 14th Divisional Signal Coy. R.E.

20/7/18.

Confidential

WAR DIARY
— of the —
14th Signal Coy R.E.

August 1918.

(Volume 39)

Army Form C. 2118.

WAR DIARY
~~INTELLIGENCE SUMMARY~~
(Erase heading not required.)

Instructions regarding War Diaries and Intelligence Summaries are contained in F.S. Regs., Part II. and the Staff Manual respectively. Title pages will be prepared in manuscript.

Place	Date	Hour	Summary of Events and Information	Remarks and references to Appendices
EPERLECQUES	1/8/18		Routine work. Setting into fresh camp. Lt A MACLEOD RE proceeded on leave.	K.
	2/8/18		do do Heavy rain.	K.
	3/8/18		2nd Army Signal Horse show BAVINCHOVE. Showery.	K.
	4/8/18		5 Representatives from Company proceeded to Army Interservice Service TERDEGHEM. Capt R.W. NEWMAN Glou'cs R. (a Signal School) proceed to CASSEL to take over Signals 30th Div' Artillery. Lecture on Aeroplane Cooperation with Infantry by Lt Col JAMES R.A.F. at MOULLE. 2 Officers 3 OR attended. Fine, cloudy.	K K K K
	5/8/18		14th Division Horse show EPERLECQUES.	K
	6/8/18		Routine work. Horses Inspection by C.O.	K
	7/8/18		Routine work.	K
	8/8/18		Routine work.	K
	9/8/18		do	K
	10/8/18		do	K
	11/8/18			K
	12/8/18		Message Carrying Rocket demonstration at INGLINGHEM 5pm. Parties from Div' Signal School, Battalions and Bde section attended	K

WAR DIARY
or
INTELLIGENCE SUMMARY.

(Erase heading not required.)

Army Form C. 2118.

Place	Date	Hour	Summary of Events and Information	Remarks and references to Appendices
EPERLECQUES	13/8/18		Routine work.	—
"	14/8/18		Major L.R. THODAY proceeded on 7 days Wireless Course 2nd Army Signal School.	—
"	15/8/18		Routine work. Lt. A. MACLEOD returned from leave.	—
"	16/8/18		Inspection of Transport, Horses & Saddlery, by G.O.C.	—
"	17/8/18		Routine work. Party sent to bathe at CALAIS.	—
"	18/8/18	to		—
"	19/8/18		Preparations Commenced for move to forward area. Advance party sent forward to COUTHOVE CHATEAU. Communication with 43 Inf Bde via 34 Div LA LOVIE	—
"	20/8/18		Transport moved at 7.15 a.m. to WORMHOUDT. Remainder of personnel moved by lorries to COUTHOVE CHATEAU. Signal Office opened at 4 p.m. at COUTHOVE CHATEAU.	—
			Signal Office at EPERLECQUES closed at 4 p.m. Divl Hqrs. COUTHOVE CHATEAU.	—
COUTHOVE	21/8/18		Transport marched from WORMHOUDT to PROVEN AERODROME.	—
"	22/8/18		Routine work. Transport moved from PROVEN AERODROME to PARDO CAMP on COUTHOVE - PROVEN Road. MAJOR L.R. THODAY returned from Wireless Course.	—
"	23/8/18		Routine work. Communication was established with 41 Inf Bde. TUNNELLING CAMP, 42 Inf Bde ROAD CAMP, GTR ST JAN-TER-BIEZEN area.	—

WAR DIARY or INTELLIGENCE SUMMARY

Army Form C. 2118.

Place	Date	Hour	Summary of Events and Information	Remarks and references to Appendices
COUTHOVE	23/6/18 Cont'd		Routine work. Communication arranged to M.G. Bn. at BLAEKERIT (MOLSHAY CAMP) Pioneer Bn. via 41 Bde Exchange. Signal School arrived at COUTHOVE.	15
"	24/6/18		Classes commenced for Signal School in Pierre Buzzy Amplifier + Loop Set.	15
"	25/6/18		Church Parade. Routine	15
"	26/6/18		Orders received to take over the line from 34th British Division with 34th Div'l Artillery. 14 Div Hqrs to remain at COUTHOVE.	15
"	27/6/18		O.C. went down line with O.C. Signals 34 Div. Arrangements made for taking over lines & transferring them from LA LOVIE (34 Div Hqrs) to COUTHOVE châlain. 41st Inf Bde proceeded to BRAKE CAMP near VLAMERTINGHE. O.C. Signals 41st Inf Bde went over left Bde sector line with O.C. Signals 103 Inf Bde. M.G. Battn moved to DIRTY BUCKET CAMP near VLAMERTINGHE.	
			Manned Test Posts of 34 Div Signals relieved by Coy men.	16
"	28/6/18		Transference of 34 Div System to COUTHOVE continued. Forward Exchange taken over.	15
"	29/6/18		14 Div took over YPRES sector from 34 Div at 3 a.m.	15
"	30/6/18		Arrangements commenced for new trunk system between VLAMERTINGHE and	15

Army Form C. 2118.

WAR DIARY
or
INTELLIGENCE SUMMARY

(Erase heading not required.)

Instructions regarding War Diaries and Intelligence Summaries are contained in F. S. Regs., Part II. and the Staff Manual respectively. Title Pages will be prepared in manuscript.

Place	Date	Hour	Summary of Events and Information	Remarks and references to Appendices
COUTHOVE	30/8/18		Been in huts, also two Brit. forward by an alternative route. Reconnoitred route for new Bivy with Corps Recce Officer.	K
	31/8/18		Reported evacuation of KEMMEL by enemy.	K

Chorley Major
O.C. 1st Div Signal Co. R.E.

31/8/18

(6392) Wt. W6192/P875 1,500,000 4/18 McA & W Ltd (E 2815) Forms W3091/4.　　　Army Form W.3091.

WR 36

A+ Q.

Cover for Documents.

Nature of Enclosures.

CONFIDENTIAL

WAR DIARY

OF THE

14th DIVISIONAL SIGNAL COY. R.E.

from 1st September — 30th September 1918.

Notes, or Letters written.

Volume

Army Form C. 2118.

WAR DIARY
or
~~INTELLIGENCE SUMMARY.~~

(Erase heading not required.)

Instructions regarding War Diaries and Intelligence Summaries are contained in F.S. Regs., Part II. and the Staff Manual respectively. Title pages will be prepared in manuscript.

Place	Date	Hour	Summary of Events and Information	Remarks and references to Appendices
COUTHOVE	31/8/18		Bdes in line also two Coys found by an alternative bn. Or next day. Ground & arranged route & proposed test areas with Corps. Burs. Officer.	
"	31/8/18		Report received of enemy evacuation of Kemmel.	
"	1/9/18		Rearranged route of new buoy. Commencing at VLAMERTINGHE CHATEAU to pass through a test point at ROME FARM sheet 28 NW 1/20000 H4a.5.5 and then to Bde Hqrs at H5c.9.9.	
"	2/9/18		Work commenced at VLAMERTINGHE CHAU with 180 men B.W.I. Regt. one company (100 men) of 6th Wiltshire Regt. Corps supply one officer & 10 O.R. a signal party to supervise work. Trench reached point about H3a.6.2.	Appendix/2
"	3/9/18		Buoy continued & reached point about shelf of road at H36.25.20. Final 440 yds tested and found correct (40 pairs)	
"	4/9/18		Buoy continued to point about H4a.2.4	
"	5/9/18		ROME FARM H4a.5.5. two infantry parties carried out WT messages carrying rockets between BORDER CAMP A3b.5.5 and VLAMERTINGHE. Results were very bad, rockets fell within 150 yds of party at VLAMERTINGHE only three fired.	
"			Bde relief. Experiments carried out with Lucas signalling lamps available nearby to	

WAR DIARY
or
INTELLIGENCE SUMMARY.
(Erase heading not required.)

Army Form C. 2118.

Place	Date	Hour	Summary of Events and Information	Remarks and references to Appendices
COUTHOVE	6/9/18		14 Divl Arty Hqrs relieved 29th Divl Arty Hqrs. Bury route continued to about H40 & 7. Capt. C. WRIGHT R.E. reported from VIII Corps Signal School to relieve CAPT S.G. ANDERSON OC SIGNALS 14th DIV ARTY. LT. R.S. TRIMBLE proceeded to 41st Inf Bde Hqrs to take over command of N° 2 Sect 14 Div Signal Co R.E. 2/LT E.E. WATSON OC N° 2 SECTION proceeded to HQrs to take over command of N° 1A Sect vice LT R.S. TRIMBLE.	
"	7/9/18		First Squad of Signal School passed out, and commenced Amplifi Buzzer and Loop set course under O/c Wireless Section. CAPT C. WRIGHT R.E. took over 14 Divl Artillery Signals vice CAPT S.G. ANDERSON R.E. who proceeded to 2nd i/c 33rd Div Signal Company. Very heavy Thunderstorm 3pm to 4.15 pm.	
"	8/9/18		Reconnoitred route for buried forward of MACHINE GUN FARM towards DEAD END - Buried route selected points midway between ROME FM and MACHINE GUN FARM.	
"	9/9/18		Tested out old disused bury between RAMPARTS YPRES and HELL FIRE CORNER and found it fair good, hear bury reached H50.0.0	

Army Form C. 2118.

WAR DIARY
or
INTELLIGENCE SUMMARY
(Erase heading not required.)

Instructions regarding War Diaries and Intelligence Summaries are contained in F. S. Regs., Part II. and the Staff Manual respectively. Title Pages will be prepared in manuscript.

Place	Date	Hour	Summary of Events and Information	Remarks and references to Appendices
COUTHOVE	9/9/18		Great difficulty experienced with work and trench falling in. Very wet. Rain storms. LT STANSFELD proceeded for duty with 64 A.F.A. Bde.	
"	10/9/18		New Bury reached H5a 5.0.	
"	11/9/18		New Bury reached point 50 yds E of MACHINE GUN FARM. Rain. 2/Lt EE WATSON proceeded on leave. Arrangements made to move to intermediate winter station at BORDER CAMP to the Ramparts YPRES.	
"	12/9/18		New Bury reached H5d F.4. 41 Bde relieved 42 Bde in left Sector.	
"	13/9/18		New Bury reached H5d F.4. 41 Bde took over too fast of the front head	
"	14/9/18		New Bury reached H6c 7.5. 41 Bde moved to SCHOOL CAMP near ST JAN TER BIEZEN. by 43 Bde. 43 Bde moved Bury reached H12 b 9.7. 2/Lt FLEMING 42 Bde moved to STEENVOORDE. Reported as supernumerary from II Corps	
"	15/9/18		Bury reached SUICIDE CORNER. Forward Exchange in BORDER CAMP closed down.	
"	16/9/18		Party of 1 NCO and 6 men sent to ORWELL CAMP to commence work on new Signal Office and burying leads. G.O.C. 14 Division held a Conference at 10 am OE Signals attended.	

WAR DIARY or INTELLIGENCE SUMMARY

Army Form C. 2118.

Place	Date	Hour	Summary of Events and Information	Remarks and references to Appendices
COUTHOVE	19/9/18		OC Signals + Asst. Officer visited 35" Divn Signals to make arrangements for transference of lines to ORWELL CAMP. 78 Partially trained Signallers sent to Battalion for duty. Linesmen. OC Signals 42 Inf Bde visited area of new Divisional front with a view to taking over on 19th. OC Signals 9th + 29th Divisions came to make arrangements for taking over from 14 Div Signals.	
"	19/9/18		Arrangements made for bringing 21 pairs from WALKER FARM to Q Test Box here DICKE BUSCH, in order to hook up rear lines with forward lines. Laying up of Q Test point in ORWELL CAMP completed. 9th Division Signals relieved all local telephones + exchange. 42 Bde moved into his at HAGUE FARM (35th Div)	
ORWELL CAMP	20/9/18		Div Hqrs moved from COUTHOVE to ORWELL CAMP 28/G/9d. 43 Bde moved from WALKER FARM 43 Bde moved to 28/H28a 2.2, 41 Bde moved to WINNIZEELE area. Party from WALKER FARM to Q Test point commenced at 7/pm. 300 lines from Pioneer Battalion digging Party with Officer from AY Cable Section Supervised work. Communication established with Corps, 42 + 43 Inf Bdes, MG Battalion. R.F.A. Bde, Division on Flanks. Div how under XIX Corps.	
"	21/9/18		Wireless station established at DIV HQRS, 42 + 43 Inf Bde Hqrs. Div Directing station moved to HAGUE FARM. Corps erected Directing station at ORWELL CAMP. Preliminary orders received for forth coming operations Signal Instructions prepared and forwarded to 14 DIV "G"	

WAR DIARY or INTELLIGENCE SUMMARY

Army Form C. 2118.

Place	Date	Hour	Summary of Events and Information	Remarks and references to Appendices
ORWELL CAMP	22/9/18		Arrangements made for the supply of Dogs and Pigeons. Exchange established at Divl Battle Hqrs. Seven pairs of cable laid from HAGUE FARM to WALKER FARM, as an alternative route to Buried System. Communication Instructions to orders re Dogs issued for forth coming operation. Copy attached.	
"	23/9/18		Communication established with BdOS. Open wires now working to DOMINION FM. Open lines transferred to W R-Q Coy. WR test point taken over by Coy, Sewing commences. Advance party proceeded to HAGUE FM to wire up office.	
"	24/9/18		41 Bde moved to HEDGE FM from OUDERDOM. Communication laid to them, also to Bomb Store OUDERDOM and Divisional Reception Camp near ABEELE.	
"	25/9/18		Open wires run through to HAGUE FM. Visual arrangements completed between Divl Adv Hqrs & 43 Bde Hqrs.	
"	26/9/18		Division moved to advanced Hqrs at HAGUE FM, H31A 7.9. Sheet 28. Taking over at 6 pm. 42 Bde moved to Hqrs at North end of DICKEBUSCH lake. H28d 6.1. 43 Bde at INDUS FM H28a 3.0. Communication established satisfactorily. Divl Rear Hqrs remained at ORWELL FM. 41 Bde Hqrs moved up to OUDERDOM area.	
HAGUE FM H31A 7.9	28/9/18		14th Division attacked with 42nd and 43rd Infantry Bdes at 5.30 a.m. Objectives being THE BLUFF, PICCADILLY FM and ST ELOI CRATERS. Division on Right (34th) and left (35th) also attacked. Reported at 9.30 a.m., all objectives taken. Communication held satisfactorily up to this hour. Heavy rain.	

Army Form C. 2118.

WAR DIARY
or
INTELLIGENCE SUMMARY
(Erase heading not required.)

Instructions regarding War Diaries and Intelligence Summaries are contained in F. S. Regs., Part II. and the Staff Manual respectively. Title Pages will be prepared in manuscript.

Place	Date	Hour	Summary of Events and Information	Remarks and references to Appendices
HAGUE FM H31a 7.9	28/9/18		Cont'd. Wireless communication proved very useful. Directing Station intercepted messages sent by French Loop Sets. Signal Section of 43 Inf Bde took 22 prisoners.	
"	29/9/18		XIX Corps moved their Hqrs to ORWELL FM, 14 Div Rear Hqrs moved to near ABEELE. 34th and 41st Division took over Divisional front. Hqrs of 14th Div + Infantry Bde remained stationary. Wireless sets drawn in.	
WARATAH	30/9/18		Div Hqrs moved to WARATAH CAMP. Bde Situated. 41st Bde RENINGHELST area. 42nd Bde, OUDERDOM area, 43rd Bde DICKEBUSCH area. Division transferred to XV Corps. Rear Hqrs moved up to WARATAH Camp. Very heavy rain.	
WARATAH	1/10/18		Communication arranged through 42 Bde Exchange, 1st took over Div Adv Signal Office at HAGUE FARM.	

Moodey Major.
O.C. 14 Div Signal Co R.E.

(6392) Wt. W6192/P875 1,500,000 4/18 McA & W Ltd (E 2815) Forms W3091/4.　　　Army Form W.3091.

Cover for Documents.

Nature of Enclosures.

Confidential

WAR DIARY

OF THE

14 DIVISIONAL SIGNAL COY RE

Period October 1918

Notes, or Letters written.

Volume 41

WAR DIARY
or
INTELLIGENCE SUMMARY

of 14th DIV SIGNAL COY. R.E.

Army Form C. 2118.

(Erase heading not required.)

Place	Date	Hour	Summary of Events and Information	Remarks and references to Appendices
WARATAH	1/10/18		41st and 42nd Inf Bdes moved to WYTSCHAETE area. Two detachments from No 11 Cable Section proceeded to KANDAHAR FARM 28/T10.b.6.8 to be ready to lay lines forward. Continental method of line came into force.	
KANDAHAR FM. 28/T10.b.8.8	2/10/18		Div Adv Hqrs moved to KANDAHAR FARM, 41st Inf Bde relieved 90th Inf Bde. Hqrs of 30th Div in the WARNETON - COMINES Sector, Bde Hqrs near MESSINES. Two overland cables laid to them. Wireless also established. 42nd & 43rd Inf Bdes less two attached to II Corps for rebuilding YPRES - MENIN road. Div Rear Hqrs remained at WARATAH CAMP. Roads very bad for D.R. motor cyclists.	
"	3/10/18		Arrangements made to Horse B/Po. Pioneer Battalion put on phone. Line laid to M.G. Battalion at LINDENHOEK. Lateral line laid to 30th Div on our left. Second cable put through to 41 Bde.	
"	4/10/18		Machine Gun Battalion moved to NEUVE EGLISE. Arrangements made to commence work on getting through on old MESSINES Tunnel route.	
"	5/10/18		Line through to 31st Div. Advanced Hqrs. on our right. Cay Office came up with Capt Tripean to KANDAHAR FM. 41st Inf Bde took over extra front on left and gave up some front on right to 31st Div. Divisional front now extends from 28/V.1.d.4.4 to 28/P.30.c.0.3.	

Army Form C. 2118.

WAR DIARY
or
INTELLIGENCE SUMMARY
(Erase heading not required.)

Instructions regarding War Diaries and Intelligence Summaries are contained in F.S. Regs, Part II. and the Staff Manual respectively. Title Pages will be prepared in manuscript.

Place	Date	Hour	Summary of Events and Information	Remarks and references to Appendices
KANDAHAR F.M.	5/10/18		Work commenced on old buried route from Test point NT (28/T6c 2.9) to Test point LD2 (28/T6b 2.9) 16 pairs found good.	
"	6/10/18		41 Inf Bde suggested moving to the vicinity of WAMBEKE, line laid to new hqrs. 235 A.T. Coy put onto Bn Exchange. Rumoured report to America by Germany for armistice and discussion of peace terms.	
"	7/10/18		Testing out old buried went from LD2 to HF (28 O 31 b 6 6) to NY (O 32 b 3 2) also HF	
	8/10/18		Ditto ditto	
			to FL (O 25 d 7.7) None of the pairs were found to be "Through"	
"	9/10/18		Rear Divisional HQRS move to CAESTRE. Signal Company wagon lines move to NEUVE EGLISE	
"	10/10/18		Training out new bury from SM (28 T 6 c 6.8) to LD3 (T 6 b 3.2) LD4 (U1a 2.2) CD.1. (U1d 4.8) M.R. (U 2 a 5.8) In LD3 and CD.1 cables were found still on trunnals and pairs were train O.K.	
	11/10/18		Working on above burine.	

2449 Wt. W14957/M90 750,000 1/16 J.B.C. & A. Forms/C.2118/12.

WAR DIARY or INTELLIGENCE SUMMARY

Army Form C. 2118.

Place	Date	Hour	Summary of Events and Information	Remarks and references to Appendices
KANDAHAR FARM	12.10.18		Working on old trenches. 43RD Brigade moved from YPRES to Sheet 28 T 5 & central. Time lost out to their Headquarters.	
"	13.10.18		Working on old trenches. 42nd Brigade moved from YPRES to Sheet 28 T 8 c.1.8. I am back from XH trenches (28.T.7.d.9.9) to their Hqrs to connect via line on [illeg] to Div Hqrs.	
"	14.10.18		Continuation of offensive by Second Army in conjunction with Belgian Army. 14th Division we asked to push forward patrols across River Lys & attack on their left was successful. This was done & their platoon crossed the river but were withdrawn in the evening.	
"	15.10.18		43rd Brigade moved up to relieve 21st Infantry Brigade. I took line from 41st Brigade Rear Headquarters at (Sheet 28 O.33.a.2.3) to 21st Brigade Hqrs (P.20.d.4.5) 41st Brigade opened advanced Headquarters at O.36.b.3.6. I extend line from their front to 21st Brigade Hqrs & obtained by wire their line to Bath Hqrs at P.26.b.4.5 which was in turn connected to 21st Brigade Headquarters. 42nd Brigade moved in to relieve 41st Brigade. Took over Rear 41st TBd Headquarters as Advanced Exchange.	
"	16.10.18		T/M Repairing and maintaining lines between Advanced Exchange & 42 & 43 Brigades.	

Army Form C. 2118.

WAR DIARY or INTELLIGENCE SUMMARY

(Erase heading not required.)

Instructions regarding War Diaries and Intelligence Summaries are contained in F. S. Regs., Part II. and the Staff Manual respectively. Title Pages will be prepared in manuscript.

Place	Date	Hour	Summary of Events and Information	Remarks and references to Appendices
KANDAHAR FARM	17.10.18		43RD Brigade moved to CHATEAU HAZEBROUCK (Sheet 28. O.31.c.5.8) MERVICQ. I line laid for GARE DIEUX Roads. To the above Headquarters 42ND Brigade advanced to le BEAU CHÊNE S. E. of COMINES. Communication maintained by line laid at day previously by 42nd Brigade to the Battalion.	
MERVICQ	18.10.18		Divisional Hqrs moved to CHATEAU HAZEBROUCK opening up at 10 a.m. I ants return line were run out to 42nd Brigade Hqrs at NEUVILLE-EN-FERRAIN and 43rd Brigade Hqr at BLANC FOUR.	
BLANC FOUR	19.10.18		Divisional Hqrs moved to BLANC FOUR at 10.00. Reeled up line laid from MERVICQ to NEUVILLE. I ant out new line to 43rd Bde Hqrs at HAUT JUDAS. also line from the 42nd Bde Hqrs at Sheet 37 A.3.a.2.1.	
BLANC FOUR	20.10.18		43rd Brigade Hqrs moved to ESTAIMPUIS. Line extended from HAUT JUDAS to the point. 42nd Brigade Hqrs moved to LUINGNE 41st Brigade moved to HERSEAUX.	
MOUSCRON	21.10.18		Divisional Headquarters moved to MOUSCRON at 14.30. I ran lead from new Headquarters to 42nd Brigade Hqrs also to 41st Bde Hqrs of new stores on to 43rd Brigade Hqrs. All Brigade Hqrs remaining in same position as yesterday.	

Army Form C. 2118.

WAR DIARY
or
INTELLIGENCE SUMMARY

(Erase heading not required.)

Instructions regarding War Diaries and Intelligence Summaries are contained in F. S. Regs., Part II. and the Staff Manual respectively. Title Pages will be prepared in manuscript.

Place	Date	Hour	Summary of Events and Information	Remarks and references to Appendices
MOUSCRON	23.10.18		42nd Brigade relieved 43rd Brigade in the line. 42nd Brigade moved their headquarters to DOTTIGNIES. Line extended from LUIGNE to the front. Held up next to D VIII line from HAUTE JUDAS to BLANC FOUR. Commenced work on open wire from MOUSCRON to railway station and along railway to HERSEAUX.	
"	23.10.18		Continued work on open wire as above. Got train through on open wire to 43rd Brigade. Also 4 pairs through from H.Qrs to railway station. Rothey is one train for 42nd Brigade + another train to Machine Gun Battalion who moved to LUIGNE.	
"	24.10.18		Continued work on open wire from DOTTIGNIES to railway and along railway towards HERSEAUX. Held in cable drawn about by roads on our wires.	
"	25.10.18		Continued work on open wire from DOTTIGNIES station along railway.	
"	26.10.18		New open wire rods laid for through from Divn to 42nd Brigade Hqrs also from 42nd Brigade Hqrs to 43rd Brigade Hqrs.	
"	27.10.18		Working on open wire route along railway from DOTTIGNIES towards HERSEAUX.	
"	28.10.18		Ditto ditto. Laid cable from 42nd Brigade Hqrs to advanced railway at TROIS FARM Sht 29 U.2.a.d.	

2449 Wt. W14957/M90 750,000 1/16 J.B.C. & A. Forms/C.2118/12.

Army Form C. 2118.

WAR DIARY
or
INTELLIGENCE SUMMARY
(Erase heading not required.)

Instructions regarding War Diaries and Intelligence Summaries are contained in F. S. Regs., Part II. and the Staff Manual respectively. Title Pages will be prepared in manuscript.

Place	Date	Hour	Summary of Events and Information	Remarks and references to Appendices
MOUSCRON	29.10.18		Repairing routes on railway from MOUSCRON - HERSEAUX - DOTTIGNIES damaged by explosion of mines. Testing power circuit from MOUSCRON - DOTTIGNIES. Working power circuit.	
Do	30.10.18		Gantry through train on railway route from MOUSCRON - HERSEAUX for 41st Brigade also another train for 43rd Brigade. Buried power circuit tested out OK from MOUSCRON - DOTTIGNIES. MOUSCRON - HERSEAUX.	
Do	31.10.18		Connecting buried circuit from MOUSCRON - DOTTIGNIES by open power circuit to High Signal Office. Testing buried route DOTTIGNIES - COYGHEM. Ruling up open cable from MOUSCRON - HERSEAUX.	

Hugh Tupper
Capt RE
o/c 14th Signal Coy RE

Army Form C. 2118.

WAR DIARY or INTELLIGENCE SUMMARY

14th DIVISIONAL SIGNAL COY. R.E.

Vol 34

(Erase heading not required.)

Instructions regarding War Diaries and Intelligence Summaries are contained in F.S. Regs., Part II. and the Staff Manual respectively. Title Pages will be prepared in manuscript.

Place	Date	Hour	Summary of Events and Information	Remarks and references to Appendices
MOUSCRON	1-11-18		Pulling through pair of lines on railway route from MOUSCRON — DOTTIGNIES for 47th Brigade R.T.A.	
"	2-11-18		Diverted cable line from DOTTIGNIES to TROIS. FMS. SW. 22 D 20d to terminal station at COYGHEM and connecting it to buried route back to DOTTIGNIES. Pulling out cable stream aroused. Testing out open wire route from MOUSCRON Station to TOURCOING Goods Station and clearing faults.	
"	3-11-18		Rigged up cable line to DOTTIGNIES. Pulling through 4 pairs on open route from TOURCOING Goods Station to Standard on church in GRANDE-PLACE.	
TOURCOING	4-11-18		Moved Divisional Headquarters to TOURCOING at 11.00. Laid 4 pair of cable for Headquarters (Sheet 36 F.10b 6.7) to Standard on church.	
"	5-11-18		Laying cable lines out from Headquarters to permanent route at Gendarmerie TOURCOING (Sheet 36 F.5 d.8.1) to 4 testing at the pairs on permanent route & clearing faults on pair to 36th Division. & The a the main for a field line.	
"	6-11-18		Testing out pair at MOUSCRON STATION POLE getting all circuits & testing them in to the hot spot on panels. Laying line from DAC Headquarters to Pioneer Battn Hqrs.	

2449 WL W4957/Mq0 750,000 1/16 J.B.C. & A. Forms/C.2118/12.

WAR DIARY
or
INTELLIGENCE SUMMARY

(Erase heading not required.)

Army Form C. 2118.

Place	Date	Hour	Summary of Events and Information	Remarks and references to Appendices
TOURCOING	7.11.18		Relaying & clearing faults on 46 & 47 Poles & lines along new lines between HERSEAUX & DOTTIGNIES	
Do	8.11.18		Traffic cable line from Pow Hours COYGHEM to ESPIERRES CHATEAU	
Do	9.11.18		Enemy retreated from the SCHELDT. 43rd Brigade moved to HEICHIN. It is noted from TROIS FMS to the new Headquarters. Divisional report centre opened at DOTTIGNIES at 15:00 and closed at 25 18:00 as awaits the advance & the maneuvering of the front the Division was engaged on"	
Do	10.11.18		43rd Brigade moved to MARCOING. Cable line laid from DOTTIGNIES station to this point. Picking up of open wires from station to the Pow station via MOUSCRON. Pow Station cut off open wires. Have a rest & back to Division.	
Do	11.11.18		Armistice came into force 11 a.m.	
Do	12.11.18		Party clearing contacts and faults on route to MOUSCRON. Major Thesley returns from leave. Capt Tapin proceeded on leave.	
Do	13.11.18		Parties reeling up cable toward BLANC FORT.	
"	14.11.18		41 Peta Hqrs moved from HERSEAUX to BONDUES. Battns situated in BONDUES area. Communication obtained on existing open wire routes.	

Army Form C. 2118.

WAR DIARY
or
INTELLIGENCE SUMMARY
(Erase heading not required.)

Instructions regarding War Diaries and Intelligence Summaries are contained in F. S. Regs., Part II. and the Staff Manual respectively. Title Pages will be prepared in manuscript.

Place	Date	Hour	Summary of Events and Information	Remarks and references to Appendices
TOURCOING	15/11/18		43 Bde moved into TOURCOING. Party laid cable to Divi. Hqrs.	
"	16/11/18		14 M.G. Battn. and 15th N. Lanc. Regt. moved into TOURCOING. Cable laid.	
"	17/11/18		Church parade and march past Army Commander at ROUBAIX. Coy sent 2 Offr and 25 O.R. 47 Bde RFA moved into TOURCOING	
"	18/11/18		Parties lifting up derelict cable in Divisional area	
"	19/11/18		do do	
"	20/11/18		Lecture on demobilisation as delivered at D.H.Q.	
"	21/11/18		Normal.	
"	22/11/18		Arrangements commenced for Military Tattoo at ROUBAIX.	
"	23/11/18		Normal.	
"	24/11/18		Normal.	
"	25/11/18		} Normal.	
"	26/11/18			
"	27/11/18			
"	28/11/18			

L. Hughes Capt RE

Army Form C. 2118.

WAR DIARY
or
INTELLIGENCE SUMMARY

(Erase heading not required.)

14th Divisional Signal Coy. R.E.

Vol 39

Instructions regarding War Diaries and Intelligence Summaries are contained in F. S. Regs., Part II. and the Staff Manual respectively. Title Pages will be prepared in manuscript.

Place	Date	Hour	Summary of Events and Information	Remarks and references to Appendices
TOURCOING	Dec 1		Maj. L. R. THODAY M/c Company left for 6 months tour of duty in England winning are for electric light Tattoo at ROUBAIX. General Routine work	
Do	2nd		Entered work at ROUBAIX. General Routine work	
"	3rd		Ditto	
"	4th		Dismantling electric lights at ROUBAIX ditto	
"	5th		Maj G.R. GRANGE arrived to take command of Company. General Routine	
Do	6th		General electric light work for Tattoo at TOURCOING. Ditto	
Do	7th		ditto ditto Capt H. TREDESS rejoined from leave	
Do	8th		Entered ditto General Routine work	
Do	9th		Ditto Ditto	
Do	10th		Finishing Ditto	
Do	11th		Dismantling electric lights re ditto Three men out today to concentration camp ditto Lt. A. ROSE returned from leave	
Do	12th		to demobilization. Two men demobilized (coalminers) General Routine work	

Army Form C. 2118.

WAR DIARY
or
INTELLIGENCE SUMMARY

(Erase heading not required.)

Instructions regarding War Diaries and Intelligence Summaries are contained in F. S. Regs., Part II. and the Staff Manual respectively. Title Pages will be prepared in manuscript.

Place	Date	Hour	Summary of Events and Information	Remarks and references to Appendices
TOURCOING	DEC 13th		General Routine work.	
Do	14th		Ditto.	
Do	15th		Ditto.	
Do	16th		Ditto. Two men left unit for demobilisation	
Do	17th		Ditto.	
Do	18th		Ditto.	
Do	19th		Sent party to COURTRAI to double cable & right return.	
Do	20th		Party consisted of 1 OPPR 12 O.R. + on billeted at COURTRAI. General Routine work. Harby tractor rolng cable in TOURCOING.	
Do	21st		Ditto.	
Do	22nd		Ditto.	
Do	23rd		Ditto.	

Army Form C. 2118.

WAR DIARY
or
INTELLIGENCE SUMMARY

(Erase heading not required.)

Instructions regarding War Diaries and Intelligence Summaries are contained in F. S. Regs., Part II. and the Staff Manual respectively. Title Pages will be prepared in manuscript.

Place	Date	Hour	Summary of Events and Information	Remarks and references to Appendices
TOURCOING	DEC 24th		General Routine	
Do	25th		Xmas day	
Do	26th		General Routine	
Do	27th		Ditto N.C.O. left unit for demobilization	
Do	28th		Ditto	
Do	29th		Ditto	
Do	30th		Ditto	
Do	31st		Ditto Two men left unit for demobilization	
			1 - Inf Napier Capt R.E.	
			14th Signal Coy R.E.	

WAR DIARY

of 1ST DIV SIG Coy. R.E Army Form C. 2118.

INTELLIGENCE SUMMARY.

(Erase heading not required.)

Instructions regarding War Diaries and Intelligence Summaries are contained in F.S. Regs., Part II. and the Staff Manual respectively. Title pages will be prepared in manuscript.

Hour, Date, Place		Summary of Events and Information	Remarks and references to Appendices
TOURCOING	JANUARY 1ST	General Return work. Salvage parties in Tourcoing area	
Do	2nd	General Return work. Ditto	
Do	3rd	Ditto	
Do	4th	Ditto	
Do	5th	Ditto	
Do	6th	Ditto	
Do	7th	Ditto. Two men left unit for demobilization	
Do	8th	Ditto	
Do	9th	Ditto	
Do	10th	Ditto. Two men left for demobilization	
Do	11th	Ditto	
Do	12th	Ditto. Two men left for demobilization	

Army Form C. 2118.

WAR DIARY
or
INTELLIGENCE SUMMARY.
(Erase heading not required.)

Instructions regarding War Diaries and Intelligence Summaries are contained in F. S. Regs., Part II and the Staff Manual respectively. Title pages will be prepared in manuscript.

Hour, Date, Place		Summary of Events and Information	Remarks and references to Appendices
TOURCOING	JANUARY 13TH	General Routine. Lt Hong went on leave	
D°	14TH	D°.tto	
D°	15TH	D°.tto	
D°	16TH	D°.tto	
D°	17TH	D°.tto	
D°	18TH	D°.tto Capt WRIGHT+ nine men left for demobilisation	
D°	19TH	D°.tto Four men left unit for demobilisation	
D°	20TH	General Routine. Coloury railway in TOURCOING + Settai Ave. Lt RADBOURNE to Ypres for duty	
D°	21ST	D°.tto	
D°	22nd	D°.tto Nine men left unit for demobilisation	
D°	23rd	D°.tto	
D°	24TH	D°.tto	
D°	25TH	D°.tto Lts A Roe left unit for demobilisation	

Army Form C. 2118.

WAR DIARY
or
INTELLIGENCE SUMMARY

(Erase heading not required.)

Instructions regarding War Diaries and Intelligence Summaries are contained in F. S. Regs., Part II. and the Staff Manual respectively. Title Pages will be prepared in manuscript.

Place	Date	Hour	Summary of Events and Information	Remarks and references to Appendices
TOURCOING	JAN 26th		General Routine. Lt MADDOX joined from "D" Corps Signal Company 2/Lt WATSON left for 14 days leave.	
"	27th		General Routine. Setting up Wireless of TOURCOING & in COURTRAI Area	
"	28th		General Routine & Setting up.	
"	29th		General Routine & Setting up.	
"	30		General Routine. Setting up an Wheels of TOURCOIN 6 & an outstation of COURTRAI	
"	31		General Routine	

Hy Tupper
Capt R.E.
4th Signal Coy R.E.

2449 Wt. W14957/M90 750,000 1/16 J.B.C. & A. Forms/C.2118/12.

Army Form C. 2118.

WAR DIARY
or
INTELLIGENCE SUMMARY 14th Div. Signal Coy R.E.

(Erase heading not required.)

Place	Date	Hour	Summary of Events and Information	Remarks and references to Appendices
	FEB 1919			
TOURCOING	1st		General Routine work. Salvage work in TOURCOING & COURTRAI Area	
Do	2nd		Ditto	
Do	3rd		Ditto	
Do	4th		Ditto	
Do	5th		Commenced demobilization of men. 10'z' animals being sent to LINSELLES Collecting Camp. 2nd Lt HOBSON & Lt TRIMBLE left for 4th Army base to England.	
Do	6th		General Routine work. Two men left for demobilization	
Do	7th		Ditto. One man left for demobilization. 9 Horses to LINSELLES	
Do	8th		Ditto. Two men left for demobilization	
Do	9th		Ditto.	
Do	10th		Ditto. Two men left for demobilization. 5 Horses to TOURCOING Collecting camp for demobilization	

Army Form C. 2118.

WAR DIARY
or
INTELLIGENCE SUMMARY
(Erase heading not required.)

Instructions regarding War Diaries and Intelligence Summaries are contained in F. S. Regs., Part II and the Staff Manual respectively. Title Pages will be prepared in manuscript.

Place	Date	Hour	Summary of Events and Information	Remarks and references to Appendices
TOURCOING	FEB 11		General Routine work. Salvage work in TOURCOING, COURTRAI area proceeding	
"	12th		Ditto	
"	13th		Ditto. LT D.L. DEANE and two men left unit for demobilization	
"	14th		General Routine work. Salvage work proceeding. Two men left unit for demobilization	
"	15th		Ditto. One man left for demobilization	
"	16th		General Routine work.	
"	17th		Ditto. Two men left for demobilization. Orders received from C.S.O. 15th Corps. to send 2 N.C.O.s & 35 O.R. to Fourth Army and 5 O.R. to Second Army	
"	18th		General Routine work. Men from Brigade instructed to hold in readiness to move off at 7.00 hrs on the 19th	

2449 Wt. W14957/M9c 750,000 1/16 J.B.C. & A. Forms/C.2118/12.

Army Form C. 2118.

WAR DIARY
or
INTELLIGENCE SUMMARY

(Erase heading not required.)

Instructions regarding War Diaries and Intelligence Summaries are contained in F. S. Regs., Part II. and the Staff Manual respectively. Title Pages will be prepared in manuscript.

Place	Date	Hour	Summary of Events and Information	Remarks and references to Appendices
TOURCOING	FEB 18th	(continued)	The orders were cancelled owing to lack of food accommodation & orders were received to send the men in not greater numbers than eight at a time. Railway Party at COURTRAI broken up.	
D.o	19th		General Ration work. Railway work in TOURCOING area.	
D.o	20th		General Ration work. LT LANG 2nd LT HOBSON returned from leave. 3 men left unit for demobilization.	
D.o	21st		Ditto. LT TRIMBLE returned from leave. LT GILBERT left for 14 days leave to England.	
D.o	22nd		General Ration work. LT STANSFELD left for 14 days leave to England.	
D.o	23rd		General Ration work. General working draft to Tenth Army. One man left unit for demobilization. CAPT H. TREPESS left for about leave to YMEREUX.	
D.o	24th		General Ration work. Eight men left for Tenth Army.	
D.o	25th		Ditto	
D.o	26th		Ditto. Continued working draft to First Army. 3 Men to LINSELLES.	
D.o	27th		General Ration work. Draft left for Tenth & Second Armies. Twelve men left unit for demobilization. CAPT TREPESS returned from leave.	
D.o	28th		General Ration work. One man left for demobilization. 12 Hours to TOURCOING cellulose works.	

H.J. Watson Capt RE
1st SIGNAL Co. RE.

Army Form C. 2118.

WAR DIARY of 14TH SIGNAL COY R.E.
INTELLIGENCE SUMMARY.
(Erase heading not required.)

Instructions regarding War Diaries and Intelligence Summaries are contained in F.S. Regs., Part II. and the Staff Manual respectively. Title pages will be prepared in manuscript.

Place	Hour, Date	Summary of Events and Information	Remarks and references to Appendices
TURCOING	MARCH 1st	General Return. Maj. G.R. GRANGE left for 14 days leave to England. Ten men left unit for demobilization.	
Do	2nd	General Return. Sent men to complete draft for South Army.	
Do	3rd	General Return. 3 N.C.O.'s left unit for demobilization.	
Do	4th	General Return. One man left unit for demobilization.	
Do	5th	Ditto	
Do	6th	Ditto. Three mules sent to Tourcoing Collecting Camp.	
Do	7th	Ditto. One man left unit for demobilization.	
Do	8th	Seven horses sent to TOURCOING Collecting Camp. General Return week.	
Do	9th	Ditto	
Do	10th	Ditto	

Sgt Turnbull

WAR DIARY
or
INTELLIGENCE SUMMARY.
(Erase heading not required.)

Army Form C. 2118.

Instructions regarding War Diaries and Intelligence Summaries are contained in F. S. Regs., Part II. and the Staff Manual respectively. Title pages will be prepared in manuscript.

Hour, Date, Place	Summary of Events and Information	Remarks and references to Appendices
TOURCOING MARCH 11TH	General Routine work	
Dº 12TH	Ditto	
Dº 13TH	Ditto	
Dº 14TH	Ditto	
Dº 15TH	Ditto	
Dº 16TH	Ditto	
Dº 17TH	General Routine work. 2ND L'AVERY left for 14 days leave in England.	
Dº 18TH	General Rowlins work	
19TH	"	
Dº	"	
31ST	"	

J.F. Trimble Lt.

Army Form C. 2118.

WAR DIARY
or
INTELLIGENCE SUMMARY 14th Div. Signal Coy
(Erase heading not required.)

Place	Date	Hour	Summary of Events and Information	Remarks and references to Appendices
TOURCOING	Apl 4		Lieut. Lang D.M. demobilized	
"	5		Capt. A.M. Maddox "	
"	2		2/Lt. Watson E.E. to Midland Div. Signal Coy	
"	10		Lieut. B. Gilbert demobilized	
"	17		Capt. H. Trepess "	
"	18		2/Lt. Stansfield to 4th Army Signals	
"	18		2/Lt. Avery to Signals 4th Area	
"	27		Lieut. S.R. Bishop joined from the 35 Div. Signal Coy	

General Routine work carried on. during the month: Stores all booked & made ready for handing in.
The Coy is on Cadre "A" footing – 33 p; No horses or mules.

Army Form C. 2118.

WAR DIARY
or
INTELLIGENCE SUMMARY

(Erase heading not required.) 14 Div April Coy RE

Vol 44

Place	Date	Hour	Summary of Events and Information	Remarks and references to Appendices
TOURCOING	May 4		Maj J.R. Grange demobilized	
"	12		2/Lt. Dobson demobilized	
"	14		Lieut Williams, 2nd Div. Signals, arrived to take over the amalgamation of the 2 Signal Coys. (14 & 2) Dep. 16 May	
"	21		The 14 Div April Coy became the 2nd Div. Signals Coy.	
"	26		Impact a/c closed with Base Centries. New a/c opened on 1 June with Command Paymaster Base.	
"	31		Two o/ranks men demobilized during the month: strength is now 2 officers + 54 O.R.	
			General Routine work continued during month, guarding stores etc.	

J Trumble

www.ingramcontent.com/pod-product-compliance
Lightning Source LLC
Chambersburg PA
CBHW060000240426
43662CB00038B/2088